Scottish Murder Casebooks

By
N. M. Lyons

Copyright © 2021, N. M. Lyons. All rights reserved.

The moral right of the author has been asserted. Apart from any fair dealing for the purposes of research or private study, or criticism or review, as permitted under the Copyright, Designs and Patents Act 1988, this publication may only be reproduced, stored or transmitted, in any form or by any means, with the prior permission in writing of the publishers, or in the case of reprographic reproduction in accordance with the terms of licences issued by the Copyright Licensing Agency.

Acknowledgements

Newspaper image © The British Library Board. All rights reserved. With thanks to The British Newspaper Archive (www.britishnewspaperarchive.co.uk).

In writing this book, I have been most grateful for the assistance given by several libraries and institutions. My thanks are particularly due to the National Library of Scotland, the John Gray Centre and the National Archives, Kew. To my family and friends, thank you for your continued support and encouragement.

Contents

Chapter 1 – 1306: Judgment at Greyfriars............................ 9
Chapter 2 – 1530: The Gilnockie Reiver............................ 16
Chapter 3 – 1765: The Principle of Justice........................ 24
Chapter 4 – 1814: Spectre of the Gallows.......................... 33
Chapter 5 – 1821: Killing of a Turnkey............................ 44
Chapter 6 – 1902: Death Dealer at Surgeons' Hall.................. 52
Chapter 7 – 1903: A Coachman's Lament............................. 67
Chapter 8 – 1923: Mercy Neither Given nor Received................ 75
Chapter 9 – 1927: The Agnes Arbuckle Mystery...................... 88
Chapter 10 – 1977: What the Butler did Next....................... 98
Endnotes 111

N. M. Lyons

Chapter 1

1306: Judgment at Greyfriars

❖ ❖ ❖

A highly romanticised ideal of Scotland emerged over the course of the twentieth century, inspired in part by literature and film. One recurring theme in this media outpouring has been the age-old struggle between Scotland and England for recognition as distinctly separate and independent nation states. Despite many falsehoods being put forward as definitive fact, Scotland is undoubtedly of distinct interest to the world for its rich and colourful history. With that in mind, Scotland of the late Middle Ages offers a diverse and often bloody point of reference to explore.

By 1290, the death of Margaret,[1] known as the 'Maid of Norway', had left the crown of Scotland in a precarious position, with multiple rivals claiming the right to succession. In a calculated attempt to avoid civil war, the Scottish barons officially requested that Edward I[2] of England, known as 'Longshanks', to act as an arbitrator. Longshanks found in favour of John Balliol[3], who had the strongest legitimate claim to the Scottish throne, although the English king established legal confirmation that Scotland was held as a feudal dependency to the throne of England. Throughout the reign of Balliol, Longshanks utilised this to

9

destabilise the Scottish crown and the legitimacy of Scotland as an independent nation.

Less than three years after becoming King of Scotland Balliol entered into a formal alliance with France at the insistence of his councillors – the beginning of the Auld Alliance.[4] The following year, Longshanks invaded Scotland and John Balliol was deposed as king.

In 1297 Andrew Murray[5] and William Wallace[6] raised a Scottish army to resist the English occupation. Under their combined leadership, the English forces were defeated at the Battle of Stirling Bridge. Murray succumbed to wounds that he received on the field of battle and William Wallace became Guardian of Scotland. In 1298 Edward Longshanks returned to Scotland and defeated Wallace and his forces at the Battle of Falkirk, effectively ending Wallace's tenure at the forefront of Scottish independence. From then on, Wallace was a hunted man and would spend the remainder of his life trying to evade English forces.

In 1302 John, the 'Red' Comyn,[7] was appointed Guardian of Scotland, a position he would hold for the next two years. Comyn slowly but surely established a formidable reputation amongst the Scottish barons after he and Sir Simon Fraser[8] defeated an English army at the Battle of Roslin in 1303.

Unfortunately, the fortunes of Scotland had become tenuous. France and England agreed peace terms and Edward Longshanks was preparing to invade Scotland once again. To alleviate a bloodbath, the Red Comyn entered into protracted negotiations with the English, which ended in an accord in February 1304. Despite the peaceful settlement, the English demanded that William Wallace be charged as a wanted man.

This led to Wallace's capture by the English in 1305 and his execution on a charge of treason, despite having never owing any allegiance to England. Consequently, in 1306,

Edward Longshanks was formally recognised as the ruler of Scotland, which, in turn, caused a chain of events with far-reaching consequences.

On 10th February 1306, the Red Comyn met Robert the Bruce, Earl of Carrick,[9] at the church of the Franciscans, the Greyfriars at Dumfries. The meeting between the two men appeared to be held in good faith as they talked before the high altar. However, enmity soon erupted between the two men as Bruce accused Comyn of treachery and struck his adversary with his sword. Bruce's followers entered the affray, inflicting multiple blows on the Red Comyn, who fell to the floor because of his injuries.

Bruce quickly left the scene with his companions and journeyed to nearby Dumfries Castle, where Edward Longshanks' justices[10] were assembled to consider state affairs. Bruce broke into this gathering and arrested Longshanks' men. Believing that his task was complete, he was confronted with the news that the Red Comyn still lived. Fearing reprisals, Bruce dispatched two trusted men to Greyfriars, where they found the Red Comyn being ministered to by the friars. Comyn had been wounded in the attack but his injuries were not life threatening. Bruce's men allowed Comyn to take confession but thereafter dragged their quarry back into the church and brutally killed him on the altar steps, staining them with blood. Comyn's lifeless body was discarded and Bruce departed Dumfries to garner support for an uprising against Edward Longshanks.

John Comyn is killed by Robert Bruce and Roger de Kirkpatrick before the high altar of the Greyfriars Church in Dumfries, 10th February 1306.
Date: Circa 1856/1857 (First Publication).
Illustration Title: Death of Comyn, *Illustration from* 'Cassell's Illustrated History of England, vol. 1: From the earliest period to the reign of Edward the IV', *new and revised edition, London, Paris & New York, Cassell, Petter & Galpin, p.330.*
Author: Henri Felix Emmanuel Philippoteaux (1815-1884).
Image Source: Public Domain.

Less than two months later, Bruce was crowned King of Scots on 25th March 1306, with the royal robes and vestments that had been hidden from the English. The bishops of Glasgow and Moray were in attendance, as were the earls of Atholl, Menteith, Lennox and Mar, while the great banner of the Scottish kings was placed behind Bruce's throne. Isabella MacDuff,[11] Countess of Buchan and wife of John Comyn, third Earl of Buchan (a cousin of the murder victim) arrived a day late for the investiture. Isabella claimed the crown for her brother, Donnchadh IV, Earl of Fife,[12] who was still a juvenile and under the control of the English. A second coronation was therefore held and Bruce was declared Earl of Carrick, Lord of Annandale and King of Scots.

After the death of Edward Longshanks, his ineffectual son, Edward II,[13] was crowned in 1307, but he lacked the strong leadership of his father. Over the course of two days in June 1314 Bruce defeated the English forces at the Battle of Bannockburn in the first war of Scottish independence. However, this victory did not bring a definitive end to hostilities between Scotland and England. This was only achieved some fourteen years later with the Treaty of Edinburgh–Northampton, signed in 1328, under the terms of which England recognised a fully independent Scotland and acknowledged Bruce and his heirs and successors as the rightful rulers of Scotland.

Scotland's long road to freedom was littered with broken agreements and war-torn battlefields, but the assassination of the Red Comyn represents a turning point in expedience. Bruce had undoubtedly formulated a plan to stake his claim to the Scottish throne but it is not clear whether the actions that he took against the Red Comyn were genuinely premeditated. After all, the location of the meeting between Bruce and the Red Comyn at Greyfriars in Dumfries should have guaranteed the safety of each man, as holy ground was deemed a place of sanctuary, precluding violence.

Scottish accounts of the time dictate that the meeting was set to enable Bruce and the Red Comyn to work in union for Scotland's freedom. The Red Comyn, however, betrayed this information to Edward Longshanks and was slain in revenge for his treachery. The English interpretation of events paints a scenario in which Bruce lured the Red Comyn to Dumfries under false pretences, where he assassinated him because he would not assent to the treason that Bruce planned against the English throne.

With the benefit of hindsight, it is easy to claim that Bruce was pragmatic and simply decided to kill Comyn to pave the way for his succession as King of Scots. That places events surrounding the Red Comyn at the heart of a coup d'état, in which Bruce would seize the throne of Scotland, go to war with England and secure Scotland's independence. Such foresight in the fourteenth century would have had to facilitate a truly remarkable chain of events when, in reality, it took the next twenty-two years for Bruce to seal Scottish freedom. However, it is just as possible that the ongoing rivalry between Bruce and Comyn and their families precipitated a spontaneous argument between the two men, which led to bloodshed. There were personal issues between the men.

In 1299, Bruce and Comyn were Guardians of Scotland and fighting in union against the English. When a dispute emerged between their followers, Comyn openly turned on Bruce and grabbed him by the throat. Yet, some years later Bruce and Comyn were also political rivals and, between 1302 and 1304, when Bruce served Edward Longshanks, the Red Comyn led the Scottish forces.

In assassinating the Red Comyn, Bruce set his life on a trajectory that could not be altered, and the once cautious and influential nobleman seriously jeopardised his own life. Bruce now faced a blood feud with the family of the Red Comyn and the renowned English forces under the unforgiving Edward Longshanks. Whatever Bruce's reasoning, the events altered both his destiny and that of his country forever.

*Melrose Abbey: Last resting place of Robert the Bruce's heart.
Image Source: Public Domain.*

Chapter 2

1530: The Gilnockie Reiver

❖ ❖ ❖

Gilnockie Tower. Location: Hollows, Canonbie, Dumfries & Galloway, Scotland.
Image Source: Public Domain.

History has shown that there is a fine line between hero and villain. The classification of these individuals can be ambiguous at best, and extremely subjective. It is essential to remember the fluidity of the borders of time – it is never enough to simply typecast a person's character. For a considered appraisal, one must look at the time and place in which a person lived, as well as the societal and cultural constraints that affected them, their own system of beliefs and, lastly and perhaps most importantly, how our own principles and prejudices influence our perceptions.

One man who has played the role of hero and villain is Johnnie Armstrong of Gilnockie, whose personality has been romanticised over the course of centuries, most notably in the works of Sir Walter Scott.[14] Armstrong was born circa 1480 in Gilnockie,[15] the youngest male child of the Laird of Mangerton, chief of the Armstrong clan.[16] Growing up in a highly volatile region, Armstrong would have had first-hand experience of countless military incursions into his homeland as invading English armies caused death and destruction. Families were torn apart and, even in relative peacetime, there was no guarantee that royal authority from either the Scottish or English crown could be relied upon to keep people safe.

From the thirteenth century onwards, Border folk sought to redress this situation. In these circumstances, a distinct group of mounted raiders known as 'Border Reivers'[17] was formed, with a rank and file consisting of English and Scots. Their task was simple – they plundered isolated and vulnerable locations in the Borders region irrespective of the north south divide if the targets had no connection to their own kinfolk.

The reivers operated a ruthless and efficient guerrilla campaign and owed loyalty to none but their own clan – their own moniker. The most prized bounties for reivers were livestock, portable valuable goods and prisoners, who could be held for ransom. Yet their most lucrative source of income came from a system of 'black rent', a sixteenth century euphemism for blackmail.

The life of a reiver was nomadic, governed as much by the seasons as by the terrain of the country, which consisted of mountainous topography and open moorland. This was inappropriate for arable farming but suited livestock grazing. Despite the onset of poor weather, the early winter calendar was the reivers' most active period as the nights were at their longest and the horses and livestock were well nourished from their summer pasture. During raiding parties, reivers would harness Irish horses, including the hobby horses,[18] or Gallow ponies – both renowned breeds for their ability to tackle inhospitable landscapes. By the sixteenth century the reivers' mode of dress included light armour such as 'brigandines' or 'jacks of plates'[19] and metal helmets. Typical weaponry included longbows or light crossbows known as 'latches', as well as small shields and lightweight lances. For close combat, a reiver relied on swords and a dagger known as a 'dirk.'

It was a rapacious way to live yet many had little choice, spurred on by the ineffectual crown systems and 'gravelkind' – a method of land tenure that divided a man's estate equally on his death between all his male children. This was a fair and equal settlement by today's standards but such that, in the sixteenth century, many people owned insufficient land to maintain themselves. In these circumstances, Armstrong quickly rose to prominence across the Anglo-Scottish border as his name became synonymous with the reivers.

He was beloved by his own kin but feared by his adversaries, who were quick to realise his undoubted skill as a strategist. However, his early years are shrouded in mystery and conjecture – perhaps the most enduring story about him is that, during his absence from his homeland, he made a considerable fortune at sea. By the 1520's, Armstrong commanded a group of men in excess of 150 and operated under the protection of Lord Maxwell[20] in a quid pro quo relationship. Armstrong operated from his own stronghold at Gilnockie Tower, situated near the country town of Langholm, and his sphere of influence stretched as far as Newcastle, over sixty miles to the east.

Such was the power of the reivers in obstructing possible Anglo-Scots diplomacy that in 1525 the Archbishop of Glasgow and Chancellor of Scotland, Gavin Dunbar, excommunicated all the so-called Border thieves from the Holy Roman Church. He decreed that a full castigation of the reivers' activities be set forth from every pulpit in the diocese and circulated throughout the Borders region. Dunbar condemned the reivers to 'the deep pit of hell, to remain with Lucifer and their bodies to the Gallows.'

Despite the ministrations of the church, it was not until the appointment of Wardens of the Marches[21] charged with keeping the peace that events came to a climax. In 1527, Armstrong raided and burned Netherby, a site now located in Cumbria, drawing the wrath of March Warden Lord Dacre,[22] who torched the Armstrong fortress at Gilnockie in retaliation.

Throughout this time, a reciprocal trade-off in violence and mayhem eventually drew young King James V of Scotland into the powerplay. Lord Dacres formally banned Armstrong and his cohorts from the town of Carlisle during daytime hours and, at that juncture, the Scottish king decided that the pervasive nature of the reivers' activities meant that all the Border lords should be imprisoned as a fitting punishment.

In June 1530, James V, supported by a large army, captured Adam Scott of Tushielaw, nicknamed the 'King of Thieves', and William Cockburn of Henderland[23] and had them conveyed to Edinburgh for summary execution. Moving south, James V sent notice to Armstrong that he would grant him a formal audience at Carlenrig.[24] While Armstrong was guaranteed safe conduct, the king was intent on a final reckoning with Armstrong and his supporters. The reason behind the King's motives can be assessed as a young monarch looking to establish his own reputation. In addition, the Scottish monarch needed to appease Henry VIII of England, who had openly demanded that the Scottish Crown deal with Armstrong, whose raiding parties south of the border represented a threat to peace between the two nations.

Armstrong rode from Gilnockie in good spirits, buoyed by what he believed would be a favourable meeting with his monarch. Dressed in fine clothing and accessories, Armstrong and his men walked into the king's camp. What was intended as a mark of respect to James V served to annoy the king as he viewed their sartorial appearance as a mark of disrespect. Despite pleading his case that neither he nor any of his men had ever harmed a fellow Scot and that his ire had been solely directed at the English, there was no appeasing the Scottish monarch.

In a final act to try and gain his freedom, Armstrong offered his unwavering fealty to the king. It was said that he shouted to the king, 'I have asked grace from a graceless face.' There was no trial for Johnnie Armstrong and his men, and the royal justice delivered was swift and merciless. The children's ballad commemorating Johnnie includes a particularly apt verse describing the antipathy of the king:

> *'Away, away, though traitor strong,*
> *Out of my sight you soon will be,*
> *I have never granted a traitor's life and I will not begin with thee.*
> *Away, away, though traitor strong,*
> *Out of my sight you soon will be,*
> *For tomorrow morning by the ten of clock*
> *You shall hang from the gallows tree.'*

While the text of the ballad does not wholly reflect the events as they are portrayed in history, nearly 500 years have passed since the time of Johnnie Armstrong and dramatic licence is inevitable. What the ballad does is demonstrate the powerful oral tradition of the people of the Scottish Borders and offer insights into one its most enduring characters. All but one of the Gilnockie reivers was hanged, and the one who avoided the noose was burnt to death for allegedly burning a small holding in which a mother and child perished. After their deaths, the bodies were buried in a deserted graveyard. Local folklore states that the trees that were used for the executions at Carlenrig simply withered away and perished.

The legend of Johnnie Armstrong of Gilnockie acts as a barometer of Scottish history during the sixteenth century. Undoubtedly, Armstrong could use the most pervasive ways and means to achieve his goals. That said, he operated in a time when equality and justice were only available to the privileged few. Armstrong and his men shared a strong feudal bond forged in poverty and continuous war – circumstances that produced a tradition of self-sufficiency.

To some, Johnnie Armstrong was a Border reiver, a simple bandit incapable of honesty and finer feelings, but to his own kinfolk he was a hero. What emerges from the action taken at Carlenrig is that the young seventeen-year-old monarch alienated the people of the Scottish Borders in an act of pure vanity.

Some twelve years later, James V of Scotland died at the tender age of thirty. In fact, he was on his deathbed at Falkland Palace when his only surviving legitimate heir was born – the future Mary, Queen of Scots. The cause of his death has never been fully explained but some say it was from a broken heart following the rout by the English forces at the Battle of Solway Moss. In the ultimate twist of fate, members of the Armstrong's of Liddesdale (Scottish Borders) sided with the English army and inflicted a fearsome defeat on the Scottish troops as they attempted to cross the River Esk at Longtown.

As for Johnnie Armstrong, high in Teviotdale, in the churchyard at Carlenrig, there is a memorial stone, which was erected in 1897. The text inscription expresses regret for Johnnie's demise: '*John murdered was at Carlenrigg, and all his gallant companie, But Scotland's heart was ne'er sae wae, to see sae mony brave men die.*'

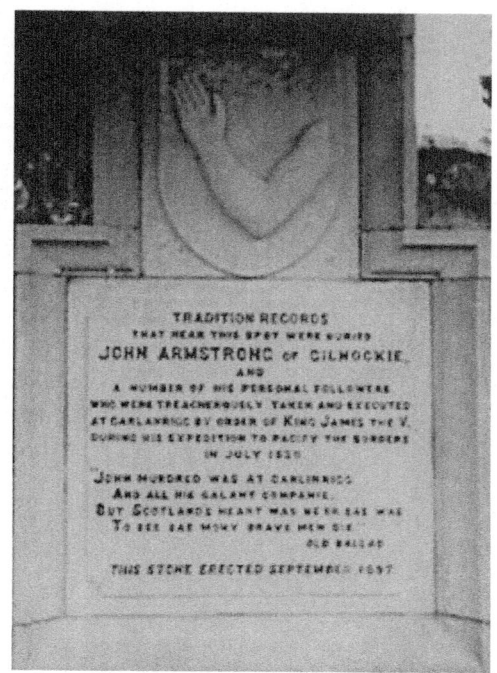

Memorial to Johnnie Armstrong and his men at Carlenrig Churchyard, Teviothead, Roxburghshire, Scotland. Image Source: Public Domain.

Chapter 3

1765: The Principle of Justice

❖ ❖ ❖

*Katharine Nairn image from an engraving at the British Museum.
Image Source: Public Domain.*

The most fundamental principle of justice, which has been widely accepted since it was first defined by Aristotle more than 2,000 years ago, is that 'equals should be treated equally and unequals unequally.'

The marriage of forty-year-old Thomas Ogilvie from East Miln, Forfar, to the much younger Katharine Nairn, the vivacious and attractive daughter of Sir Thomas Nairn of Dunsinane, was always going to be a problematic union. The marriage took place on 31st January 1765 and united two people suited in neither age nor temperament. On entering the family home, Katharine Nairn[25] must have wondered what she had let herself in for. The father of this very unfortunate family was a captain in Bonnie Prince Charlie's army in the 1745 Jacobite rebellion. Taken prisoner after the Jacobite campaign failed at Culloden in 1746, he languished in Edinburgh Castle as a prisoner for the next five years. On trying to escape over the castle walls in 1751, Captain Ogilvie fractured his skull.

Various tragedies befell the siblings of Katharine Nairn's husband. His oldest brother hanged himself; while another brother, William, was a carpenter in the navy and was crushed to death aboard ship. Of his remaining family members, his youngest brother, Andrew, a student in Edinburgh, entered a marriage with a woman of the lowest order, while Patrick, a lieutenant in the 89 Regiment of Foot, was invalided home from the East Indies. Despite this muted beginning to the marriage, however, genuine warmth appeared to exist between Thomas and Katharine if only for the briefest of moments.

Early in the couple's union, Miss Anne Clark, a cousin of the family, arrived for a visit, ostensibly to fashion a reconciliation between Alexander Ogilvie and his family after his impromptu marriage. Unbeknownst to the family, Anne had enjoyed an intimate relationship with Alexander and there was genuine malice behind her apparent role of peacemaker. Given Patrick's poor health, Anne was acutely aware that if Thomas Ogilvie failed to provide an heir, it was a credible possibility that young Alexander could inherit East Miln.

Anne became firm friends with Katharine in a short space of time and was a trusted confidante – so much so that, in Anne's own words, Katharine openly talked to her about poisoning her husband because she hated him so much. Ever the dutiful friend, Anne offered to procure the poison for Katharine.

However, before Anne could source the poison, a rumour emerged that scandalised the house relating to a perceived infidelity between Katharine and Patrick. This coincided with a financial dispute between Thomas and Patrick over the balance of money bequeathed to Patrick by his father, which had not been forthcoming. The brothers discussed this on 23rd May 1765 and, in a heated exchange, Thomas referred to Anne's allegations about the improper relationship between Katharine and Patrick. It appears that Patrick Ogilvie received the money and departed East Miln. Katharine wrote to Patrick Ogilvie and pleaded with him to return to the family home, but, in a calculated act of cruelty, the young officer flatly refused the invitation.

According to Anne, the young bride was perplexed that Anne had not provided the poison as she had promised. That same day, Anne managed to engage a doctor in conversation on the effects of laudanum and what would constitute a fatal dose. As a result of further correspondence between Katharine and Patrick it emerged that, while absent from East Miln, Patrick had managed to procure 'a small phial glass of laudanum and betwixt half an ounce and an ounce of arsenic.'

On 5th June 1765, a parcel containing the poison was delivered to East Miln for Katharine Nairn. Later that day, Thomas informed Andrew Stewart, the brother-in-law of

Thomas Ogilvie and purveyor of the package, that he had been unwell for some time and was going to consult a doctor. This information confirmed Andrew Stewart's fears about possible poisoning, as Anne had informed him that he had delivered 'black drugs' into the hands of Katharine.

On travelling home that evening from a supper party that the four had attended, Anne warned Thomas that, 'his life was threatened by his own wife' and begged him to leave home. Thomas said that he was unable to do so, but promised to accept no food or drink from Katharine's hands. Thomas would undoubtedly have been reluctant to take Anne's advice as he could not help but distrust her and question her motives. As the conversation developed, Katharine was walking beside Andrew Stewart, separated from her husband by only a short distance. She complained to Andrew that she was extremely unhappy and, 'wished her husband dead, or, if that could not be, she wished herself dead.'

The very next morning, at breakfast, Katharine poured a cup of tea from the teapot, put sugar and milk in it, and took it to her husband, who was still in bed as he had been unwell overnight. Despite working that morning, Thomas Ogilvie was taken violently ill in the kitchen and had to be conveyed to bed. At first, Katharine attended to her husband but, from lunch until his death at nine in the evening, Anne Clark ministered to the patient. In his final hours of life, Thomas Ogilvie experienced violent spasms in his bowels, vomiting and excruciating pain. After less than four months of marriage, Katharine Nairn was widowed. Patrick Ogilvie quickly instigated funeral preparations for his elder brother, unaware that Anne Clark had written to Alexander Ogilvie and communicated her fears over the death, intimating that she believed it to have been caused by poisoning.

Despite his youth, Alexander set out for East Miln, determined to find out what had happened to his brother. He was ably supported by two surgeons and the undersheriff of Forfar. The surgeons decided against a post-mortem as Thomas Ogilvie had been dead for six days by this time, and they were wary of a noxious emanation from the rapidly decaying body. Despite no tangible evidence against Katharine Nairn or Patrick Ogilvie, both were formally arrested and taken into custody at the prison in Forfar before being transported to Edinburgh to await trial at the High Court of Justiciary.

As these events progressed, Anne Clark kept herself hidden from the authorities but, on 3rd August 1765, she surrendered herself to the Lord Advocate. She and two servants from East Miln were committed to Edinburgh Castle to prevent any attempt to escape and avoid giving their testimonies to the court. When the official proceedings got underway on 5th August 1765, the judges present were the Lord Justice Clerk (Sir Gilbert Elliot of Minto), Lords Auchinleck, Alemore (Andrew Pringle), Kames (Henry Home), Pitfour (James Ferguson) and Coalston (George Broun).[26] The remaining judicial representation included the Lord Advocate (Thomas Miller of Barskimming, the Solicitor General (James Montgomery), Sir David Dalrymple (the future Lord Hailes).[27]

The indictment against the prisoners was read out and the witnesses and jury were confirmed before the court, before the case was adjourned to the following Monday, to commence at eight o'clock in the morning. In the intervening week, the defence petitioned the court for Anne Clark to be separated from the two servants in case she tried to influence their testimonies. Although the court approved this, Lord Beauclerk[28] returned Anne Clark to her previous place of confinement as he had been advised that her new lodging was unsafe and that she might attempt to abscond.

The trial got underway on 12th August 1765 and was a protracted affair, continuing uninterrupted till three o'clock on the Wednesday morning, when the jury retired to consider the evidence. Some thirteen hours later, they returned and gave a guilty verdict for both prisoners. Accordingly, the Lord Advocate deemed that sentencing should take place. This was opposed by the defence counsel, who cited 'several informalities' in the trial, challenging the validity of the verdict because they contradicted the principles of Scottish law. On this point of law, a debate ensued, climaxing in the Lord Justice Clerk stating that, 'unless a special plea was stated in arrest of judgement, he would pronounce sentence.'

It was agreed that written arguments would be submitted the following day, yielding no further movement in the case. It was suggested to the court that Mrs Nairn was with child but how far her pregnancy had advanced was not detailed. After taking medical advice from a matron, it could not be established if Mrs Nairn was pregnant. Consequently, the sentence against her was suspended until November, when her situation could be reassessed.

The decision against Patrick Ogilvie was passed and it was agreed that he was to be executed on 25th September 1765 in the Grassmarket, Edinburgh. His family tried to exert what pressure they could to win a reprieve for him. Counsellor McCarty contested that a right of appeal should be allowed via the House of Lords. However, this was to no avail as the Lord Advocate stated that the decision of the Court of Justiciary was binding.

With all avenues of appeal exhausted, Patrick Ogilvie was attended by two clergymen and members of his family on the day before his execution. To the end of his life, Patrick

Ogilvie insisted that he was completely innocent in his brother's death. As he faced the gallows on 13th November 1765, he said aloud, 'I adhere to my former confession, and die an innocent man.' He was then executed, and his body delivered to a surgeon for dissection.

As for Katharine Nairn, she was eventually found to be pregnant, and gave birth to a girl on 27th January 1766 at the Tolbooth Prison, Edinburgh, but the girl died within two hours of her birth. An execution order was then passed on Katharine, but, aided by an old family servant, she managed to escape dressed as an officer. Nearly a full day passed before the escape was noticed and, by then, Katharine Nairn was on her way to London. On arrival, she chartered a Dutch fishing boat to transport her to Holland, but, unfortunately, because of particularly bad weather, the vessel had to put her ashore on the Kent coast. The authorities sent to return her for execution assumed that she had escaped abroad from the port of Dover on another ship, although no evidence exists to determine her fate.

Conjecture at the time stated that Katharine Nairn made her escape to France and then on to America, and that she lived to be an old woman and enjoy a happy life with her Dutch husband and children. Another supposition was that she repented for her sins and became a nun, before surviving the French Revolution and returning to live in England, where she died early in the nineteenth century.

The holy orders story might be the closest to fact as an article in the *Westminster Magazine* of 1777 states that, 'Mrs Ogilvie, who escaped out of an Edinburgh gaol for the murder of her husband, is now in a convent at Lisle, a sincere penitent.' Alexander Ogilvie became the new master of East Miln but this proved to be a poisoned inheritance, as he was arrested for bigamy on 1st March 1766.

At his trial on 4th August 1766, Alexander pleaded guilty to the charge and was banished for seven years. He was, however, allowed to remain in Scotland for two months to settle his affairs. Unfortunately, while leaning over the window of a house in one of Edinburgh's tenements, 'he lost his balance, fell out, and was killed on the spot. Thus, only Anne Clark and old Lady Eastmiln withstood the changes of that eventful year.'

In conclusion, the outcome of this case created two polarising outcomes. While Patrick Ogilvie paid the ultimate price, Katharine Nairn avoided the hangman. Anne Clark was undoubtedly at the centre of events from beginning to end. Her witness testimony lasted for eight hours and was heard behind closed doors. Perhaps she exerted her force of will over Katharine Nairn and guided her actions. While there is a case for this, Katharine arguably had a strong character and quite miraculously helped to engineer her own escape.

The prosecution asserted that Thomas Ogilvie was poisoned, yet the medical professionals failed to support this with evidence. Dr Meik, who was first to attend the body, noted that the 'nails and a part of the chest of the deceased were discoloured and the tongue had swollen to an unnatural size and was fixed rigged against the roof of the mouth.' Meik was 'unacquainted with the effects of poison' but, after being told by Alexander Ogilvie that poison had been administered, he 'conjectured' that this had caused the death.

Dr Ogilvie (no family relation) who was charged with examining the body for the authorities, noted that the 'face, the arms, and several other parts of the body were black and livid, and that the nails were remarkably black.' This cannot be used as evidence of poisoning, rather showing that the corpse had been open to the elements for six days, meaning that the blackening was a result of putrefaction.

Patrick Ogilvie's purchase and supply of arsenic represents the most potent evidence for murder, yet it must also be noted that Thomas Ogilvie, although prone to hypochondria, was one of those strange enigmas – a hypochondriac who was unwell. His mother, family, friends and servants all noted to the court that, in recent years, he had endured poor health. Perhaps the poison was never administered and Thomas Ogilvie died of some undiagnosed ailment, but, then again, Katharine might well have carried out an act of mariticide.

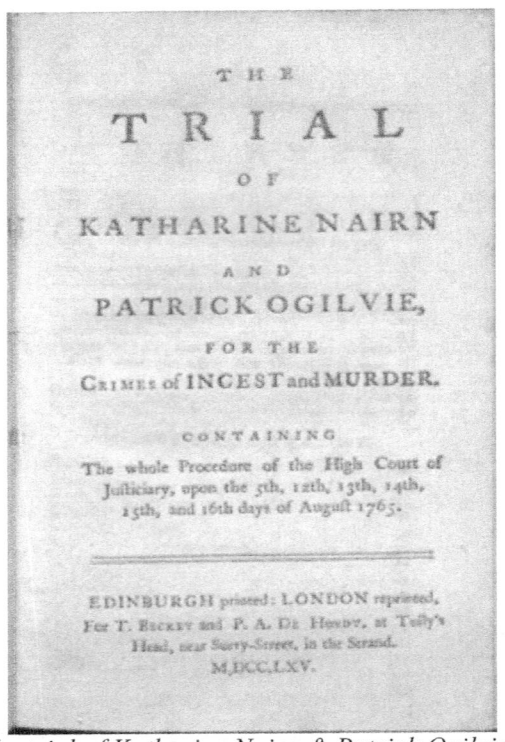

The trial of Katharine Nairn & Patrick Ogilvie. Image Source: Public Domain.

Chapter 4

1814: Spectre of the Gallows

❖❖❖

Drawing of Lord Gillies trial judge by Robert Scott Moncrieff.
Image Source: Public Domain.

The Circuit Court of Justiciary[29] was opened on Friday 8th April 1814 in Jedburgh by the Right Honourable Lord Gillies,[30] one of the Lords Commissioners on this circuit. The diary of the court began with the trial of John Gibson (a nailor by trade),[31] accused of murdering his wife, Janet Gibson, at the family home in Hawick on 19th November 1813. The indictment stated that the prisoner had entered a plea of not guilty and, with no objection set forth, a jury was sworn in and the Crown prosecution commenced.

Robert Douglas, a surgeon from Hawick, detailed to the proceedings that, on the afternoon of 19th November 1813, he was called to examine the body of the deceased. On examining Janet Gibson, he formally declared that life had been extinct for several hours. There were three distinct wounds to the windpipe of the victim. The primary incision was a deep cut from the trachea across to the left side of the neck. The laceration had cut to such a depth that it had completely separated the jugular vein and carotid artery on the side of the neck. Douglas stated that the scene of crime appeared to have recently been washed but that clear evidence of the atrocity remained, with blood on the bed linen and under the bed. Asked by the prosecution counsel what type of instrument could have inflicted the mortal wounds, the clinician indicated that the penknife presented before the court had a suitably sharp edge to have caused such injuries. Under cross-examination, Douglas observed that the deceased must have been in bed or in a reclining position when the main wound was inflicted.

Next to be put under oath was John Brook, a stocking maker by trade, who occupied a room in the upper garret storey of the house of Gideon Renwick, the father of the deceased. Brook noted to the court than he was acquainted with Gibson and his wife and had found them to be decent neighbours. On the evening preceding the murder, Brook heard the accused and his wife quarrelling, but the noise did not persist. Early the following morning, between the hours of three and four o'clock, Brook was awakened from a deep sleep by screams, which he initially believed came from some soldiers who also lodged in the house arguing with their wives.

Brook decided to investigate the disturbance and went downstairs, where he met a woman carrying a child. She said to him, 'Gibson has murdered his wife.' Alarmed, Brook proceeded to Gibson's room, where he found the door half open. On entering, he found the plaintive standing in his nightshirt and saw blood on both the floor and bed. Brook asked Gibson, 'What have you done?' The accused answered 'Frenchman! Frenchman!' Brook replied, 'It is not a Frenchman, but you have done it.'

Gibson said, 'Yes, I have murdered her, and meant to have done the same to myself, but I will now let that alone, yet I will have to die for it.' The witness clarified to the court that he understood that Gibson had become jealous of a perceived familiarity established between his wife and a French officer. Brook then left the accused in the custody of one of the soldiers while he went to fetch the police. Once Brook had familiarised the authorities with the situation, he returned to the location of the slaying with John Gordon, the Sheriff Officer. When Gordon entered the room, he said to Gibson, 'What have you done?' Gibson answered, 'Yes, I have sold her to the Frenchman now.' The defendant was then asked what instrument he had used to carry out the murder, to which he replied that he had used a broken knife, which was now on the floor of the room.

Brook was presented with the exhibit during his testimony and stated that, to the best of his knowledge, it was the same weapon that the Sheriff Officer removed from the floor of the murder scene. Brook concluded his evidence by confirming that he had then accompanied Gibson and the Sheriff Officer to Jedburgh Sheriff Court.[32] On the journey, the accused yet again declared his culpability in the death of his wife. John Gordon, a Sheriff Officer and a constable in Hawick, supplied the next deposition to the proceedings. He corroborated the evidence provided by John Brook and stated that on interviewing John Gibson he declared, 'What is done cannot be undone' and 'I have sold her, or I have sent her to the Frenchman.'

Next to take the stand was Gideon Gibson, the son of the accused, yet the defence counsel objected to this on account of the father and son relationship and on the grounds that the child was under twelve years of age. The prosecution reiterated that it was not their intention to put the child under oath but submitted to the judge that he was entitled to his witness testimony. The judge rejected any objection to the child's testimony on account of the peculiar circumstances of the case, leaving the decision with the boy, providing that he wished to give evidence. Gideon Gibson declared his intention to appear before the court to provide an account of the events that took place on the evening of his mother's death, but the prosecution counsel persisted in hearing from the child then declined to proceed with any form of questioning.

James Turnbull, a shoemaker from Hawick, then offered his attestation to the court. He noted that he had lived in a room in the same house as the Gibson family since 1812 and that he knew the husband and wife very well. On the evening of the deadly assault, Turnbull confirmed that a quarrel had taken place between John and Janet Gibson. The witness stated that he had gone down to Gibson's room but was ordered away.

Sometime later, the heated exchange intensified and Mrs Gibson cried out 'murder'. He rushed back downstairs to find the accused holding his wife's head under his arm, repeatedly striking her in the face.

As the case unfolded, it emerged that John Gibson was a native of Ayr. Born in 1774, he maintained a family tradition by taking up a trade and working as a nailor. By the age of twenty-one Gibson was a soldier in the 91st Regiment of Foot, the Argyllshire Fencibles[33] when he arrived in Hawick in 1795. This military deployment was instigated at the behest of the British Government, who were worried about antecedent behaviour that might emerge amongst the workers of Scotland, buoyed by the events of the French Revolution. There was a credible threat of civil disobedience taking effect, as the Friends of the People[34] played an increasingly active role in voicing the needs of the working man in Scotland.

When John Gibson arrived in Hawick, he was billeted in the house of the local butcher, Gideon Renwick. This proved to be a fortuitous moment in the life of the young soldier as he took an immediate liking to Renwick's twenty-one-year-old daughter Janet and, within the year, the couple were married. Despite the auspicious beginnings to the marriage, the young couple followed a nomadic lifestyle. John Gibson had subsequent postings to Lanark, Berwick upon Tweed and Ireland in 1798 as part of the forces sent to quell the Irish rebellion under Wolfe Tone's[35] United Irishmen.

Throughout the early years of their marriage, Janet followed her husband to his different postings but after the birth of their fourth child she returned home to Hawick. During Janet's time away from home she endured significant hardships, including poor housing and sanitary conditions. She also tragically lost all three of her young children.

John Gibson himself returned to live in Hawick full time in 1802 and carry on his trade as a nail maker. Unfortunately, whether through his own choice after a night of heavy drinking or by subterfuge, Gibson found himself re-enlisted in the army. He subsequently deserted and, over the next few years, lived a life on the run, managing to evade capture by living at different times in Ireland and Newcastle. However, he was pressganged while staying in Newcastle and had to jump ship to avoid serving in the British Royal Navy.

On returning to his native Scotland, Gibson set up business in the Scottish Borders towns of Langholm and Kelso with his wife and surviving children. However, it did not take long for the military authorities to trace him and he was arrested and formally charged with desertion. Janet Gibson travelled over 180 miles to her husband's place of incarceration in Aberdeen and pleaded his case. Such were the heartfelt words put forth by Janet that her husband avoided a formal sentence. However, he had to remain in army service until 1809.

Having been discharged from army service, John Gibson was again arrested, this time for desertion from the Royal Navy. As before, his good character was attested to through his hard work and attachment to his wife and children. Yet again this proved successful and the authorities were quick to release Gibson from custody. By 1812 Gibson was living with his wife Janet and their surviving eight children in the locus of Millport, within the town of Hawick. Life for the family should have been settled but this was far from the case.

As the end of the Napoleonic Wars approached, Scottish border towns played host to an ever-increasing number of

French prisoners of war. By 1812 some 120 French officers were billeted in Hawick, which brought a flash of Gaelic colour to the town. The French army personnel were afforded a great deal of autonomy and duly embraced their new home, providing concerts, opening cafés and trying to fuse their own culture with the spartan lifestyle of the Scottish Borders.

While the defence case progressed, it emerged that John Gibson was convinced that his wife had entered a clandestine affair with one of the French army officers, leading him to question the paternity of their seven-month-old baby boy. However, Gibson put forward a far more serious allegation to the court, declaring that his wife Janet had tried to poison him. In the week before the death of Janet Gibson her husband had complained that she had contrived to instigate an argument and would then refuse to sit down and share an evening meal. On the evening of the murder John Gibson stated that, 'he saw his wife sneer at him and immediately felt himself gripped with a more severe pain than he had previously experienced.' He said to his wife, 'you are trying to poison me', and reported that she laughed but made no reply.

Gibson conceded to the court that he exchanged some angry words with Janet but that this did not persist and he went to bed at around ten o'clock in the evening, sometime after his wife. Gibson noted that he was, 'in disorder both in body and mind' because they had failed to settle their issues. Awoken in the early hours of the morning, he thought he had seen a Frenchman in the room but could not find anyone. Returning to bed, he fell back asleep but awoke later with a raw thirst and asked his wife Janet to get him a glass of water, a request she refused. Gibson decided to get up but, as he did so, he was startled by his wife, who followed him out of bed and launched a furious attack, clutching him by the throat. Fearing for his life because he could not dislodge his wife's hands from his throat, he managed to get hold of his penknife and stabbed his wife in the throat, at which point her body went limp.

As the defence case rested, it appeared to all that John Gibson was resigned to his fate. His feelings proved accurate as the jury swiftly returned a guilty verdict to the court. Passing sentence, Lord Gillies stated that, 'the prisoner should be fed on bread and water until the 12th of May when, between the hours of two and four in the afternoon, he should be hanged by the executioner on a gibbet until he was dead.'

John Gibson found a sort of contrition in his final days. When he emerged from his prison cell in Jedburgh on the day of his execution he was clutching a Bible in his hand, with a local minister in proximity. Gibson was accompanied by the local magistrate and provost as well as the entire town guard – a company of some seventy men – and the group made the journey of around a mile to Bergress Sla on the outskirts of Jedburgh. At this point Gibson was placed into the custody of the Roxburgh yeomanry, under the stewardship of the Sheriff of Roxburgh.

There, the guilty man was placed in an open cart and the cortege began Gibson's long final journey to the execution site in Hawick. It must be remembered that the procession of the criminal to the gallows was intrinsic to the overall execution trial. Gibson would have encountered large crowds on his journey, as local businesses and shops closed to enable the public to view the condemned man.

As Samuel Johnson noted, 'the old method of execution was most satisfactory to all parties; the public was gratified by the procession, the criminal supported by it.' As Gibson made his way to the Common Haugh,[36] where he was to be hanged, he was joined by many of the foremost citizens of

Hawick, including the magistrates and the officiating cleric, as two detachments of yeomanry lined the road and the militia played 'The Dead March'.

Gibson's case proved to be the final public hanging to take place in Hawick. Unlike many such occasions, it was not marked by public unrest. Indeed, the proceedings had an air of a true solemnity. The guilty man ascended the scaffold and addressed the attending public as follows: 'A great many lies have been circulated about me, the authors of which I entirely forgive. I am now on the brink of eternity and I can certainly say that I never materially injured man or woman, but my own family, for which I am now to suffer […] I now warn all that are here to beware of any excessive drink or passion; to these I owe my unhappy fate.' Gibson then took his final steps to the gallows and met the justice of the executioner.

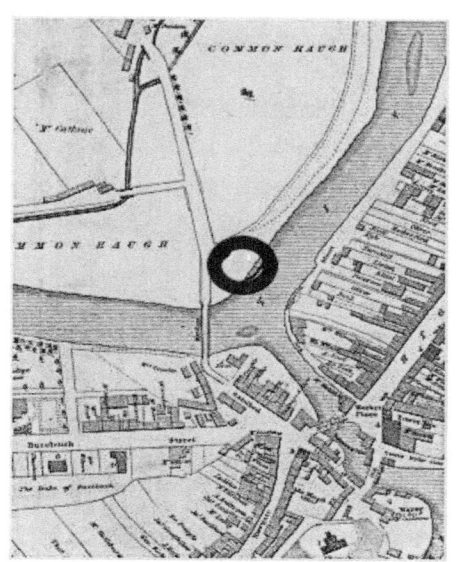

Map of the Common Haugh area outside of Hawick. Place of execution of John Gibson 1814.
Image Source: Public Domain.

In the immediate aftermath of the execution, a biographical pamphlet was issued, which provided little new information on the case except to reinforce the fact that Gibson's confession and the burden of proof was overwhelming, albeit that he might have been mentally unbalanced at the time of the killing. Such pamphlets, alongside written broadsides, were a peculiar oddity as they detailed the lurid nature of such cases, providing entertainment to the mass public both in fiction and real life. As *Punch* magazine wryly noted, 'We are a trading community – a commercial people. Murder is, doubtless, a very shocking offence; nevertheless, as what is done is not to be undone, let us make our money out of it.' Fortunately, this publication was far more lugubrious in tone and the proceeds were given to charity.

This case should have been consigned to a tragic historical footnote but three years later a startling revelation emerged. An ex-soldier under sentence of transportation for another crime provided a statement in which he claimed responsibility for murdering a woman in Hawick in December 1814. The judicial authorities in Hawick passed on the information to the Secretary of State, stating that, on the evening of the killing, a group of soldiers was passing through Hawick and sought shelter in the house where John Gibson and his family resided.

This information raises far more questions than it can ever answer. Did John Gibson kill his wife Janet, or did he wake from a troubled sleep and in a melancholy state witness his wife being murdered. Worse still as a suggestion, was John Gibson so unbalanced that he genuinely believed that he had carried out the atrocity himself? Undoubtedly, John Gibson's son Gideon, a child of only ten years old, could have provided key evidence but the Crown changed their mind on his testimony and successfully argued that it was inadmissible. What, too, of Gibson's father-in-law, Gideon Renwick Snr? The father of the victim remained silent throughout the trial and was never requested to appear as a witness. There was animosity between John Gibson and his father-in-law – Gibson felt that he deserved a share in a property that was not forthcoming. Was Gideon Renwick culpable in his complete silence?

Ultimately no further action was taken – the conviction was deemed to be sound and history will remember John Gibson as having murdered his wife. Perhaps the words of Gibson most accurately demonstrate his feelings of guilt. He stated, 'I wish to draw a veil over the events of that dreadful night. I had hardly committed the horrid deed, when the remembrance of her long-continued kindness to me rush upon my mind...' The final public hanging to take place in the Scottish Borders occurred thirty-five years after the Gibson case in Jedburgh in 1849.

After the merriment of the St Boswells Fair[37] a riot took place, involving Irish navvies who were laying the track for the Kelso railway system. Following two days of hostilities, the riot was quelled, but, unfortunately, a man who had aided the authorities in bringing a resolution to the lawlessness died from head injuries.

The trial involved three defendants and one of these, John Wilson, was found guilty and faced the gallows on 25th October 1849 in front of 3,000 onlookers. In a twist of fate, just as in the case of John Gibson, another possible conclusion to a killing emerged. Thousands of miles away in America, a deathbed confession was taken from a man who stated his involvement in the St Boswells Fair tragedy in which he admitted swapping clothes with his friend to avoid justice.

Chapter 5

1821: Killing of a Turnkey

❖❖❖

*The Life & Adventures of David Haggart 1821.
Image Source: National Library of Scotland.
Licence: CC BY-SA 4.0*

For David Bryan, his arrest and conviction for pickpocketing was part and parcel of his so-called profession. In April 1821, Bryan found himself in Kilmainham Prison, Dublin, where he awaited transportation to New South Wales to begin a sentence of penal servitude. Kilmainham was particularly busy that Easter as two notorious prisoners were in resident – Bridget Butterly and Bridget Ennis[38] – who became the last women to be hanged there. Bryan had resigned himself to his fate but, unbeknown to him, a local magistrate who was a frequent visitor to the gaol had recognised Bryan's description from the recent edition of the *Hue and Cry* newspaper.[39]

Thanks to the vigilant magistrate, it emerged that David Bryan was in fact David Haggart, a notorious fugitive from Scotland. Haggart had been declared an outlaw several months earlier after being accused of attacking Thomas Morrin, a turnkey[40] at Dumfries Prison, during his escape, leading to the man's death. Haggart was born at Golden Acre near Edinburgh on 24th June 1801 and came from a respected working-class family. However, he failed to embrace his education and was much happier out and about in the countryside with his father, helping him in his estate work as a gamekeeper and dog trainer. Although ostensibly Haggart left school to work with his father, this did not materialise, and he began to associate with shady characters on the periphery of crime. Haggart decided that it was easier to live off his earnings as a pickpocket and thief, much to the disappointment of his family.

After an alcohol-soaked adventure, Haggart duly found himself enlisted in the Norfolk Militia as a drummer but could not adapt to the rigidity of army life and left in 1814 after only one year of service.

He returned to his family full of good intentions and, for the best part of two years, he managed to keep to his word and worked as an apprentice to a millwright and engineering company. However, the company closed and Haggart could not maintain his endeavours. Before the age of twenty he embarked on a career as a violent offender – a recidivous criminal of the first order. Over the next five years, Haggart based himself in the north of England and the Southern Uplands of Scotland, working a criminal circuit by following travelling fairs and attending sporting events such as horse racing meetings. No crime was beneath him and, while he still utilised his skills as a pickpocket, he developed expensive tastes, financed by break-ins and working as a footpad thief.[41]

Throughout this period of Haggart's life, the crimes he perpetrated continued to escalate, as did the violence to which he readily resorted. While in Durham Prison in 1818 under one of his assumed names, Haggart was sentenced to death for burglary. Aided by several convicts, he took a turnkey prisoner, tied him up, gagged him and managed to scale the wall of the prison and escape to freedom. Despite this audacious prison break, he was recaptured at the Port of Leith near Edinburgh in March 1818. Yet again he proved to be a resourceful individual and stole a file, managing to cut through his leg irons and a stone from the perimeter wall to escape.

Unfortunately, Haggart could not control his violent tendencies and, while awaiting his appearance at Dumfries Court on a charge of burglary, he bludgeoned a turnkey named Thomas Morrin to death, inflicting several blows to his head and fracturing his skull. Haggart managed to fashion an escape and got himself onto a ship bound for Ireland. Reestablishing his criminal endeavours in Belfast, he was betrayed by a criminal cohort and arrested by the police.

Once again, Haggart escaped – he proved to be far more adept at evading the authorities than he was in his criminal pursuits. Over the next few weeks, he travelled through Ireland, relying on his pickpocketing skills to keep him fed and clothed. However, at a county fair at Castle William, his luck finally ran out. Trying to pickpocket a local pig farmer, he was summarily caught and held at Downpatrick Prison.[42] Unable to fashion an escape this time, Haggart had to bide his time, although he did take part in a mini blockade in his cell.

When the police authorities in Dumfries were made aware of the magistrates' suspicions over the identity of David Bryan, a police officer named John Richardson was called on to travel to Dublin and formally identify the prisoner. Haggart was returned to Scotland and went on trial for the killing of Thomas Morrin on Monday 11th June 1821. He entered a plea of not guilty, and the first witness to give evidence against him was Thomas Hunter, keeper of Dumfries Gaol. In his testimony, the witness outlined an area of the prison known as the 'cage'. Located on the second floor of Dumfries Gaol, the cage, despite its rather stark name, was neither uncomfortable nor disliked by the prisoners. Indeed, it was the most hygienic area of the prison, affording the inmates fresh ventilated air and access to a toilet.

At lunchtime on the day of the escape there were three inmates in the cage – John Simpson, serving a sentence on a charge of vagrancy, Haggart and Dunbar, who were both awaiting trial. Hunter provided the men with their meals and left them at just before quarter to two in the afternoon. John Simpson then testified that Haggart had smuggled a large stone into the cage, hidden in a canvas bag, which could be used as a weapon. At this time, the turnkey, Thomas Morrin, had been taking food to a prisoner in an adjacent cell and Dunbar requested him to unlock the cage as he wanted to return to his own cell.

Once he did this, Haggart struck the prison officer multiple times on the head with the bag containing the stone. Haggart then took Morrin's keys and the men escaped.

A servant from the kitchen named Mary Gracie corroborated Dunbar's testimony concerning his request to return to his cell. Seconds later she heard the vicious attack and Simpson shouting, 'Murder! Murder! Haggart is out and he has killed Thomas.' On stepping out of the kitchen to see what help she could provide to the injured man, Gracie was confronted by the fleeing prisoners. She let out a scream of 'Murder!' but was unable to stop the prisoners from escaping as Haggart threatened her with violence.

Both prisoners managed to escape but only Haggart got away cleanly, as Dunbar was captured a short distance from the gaol. John Jardine and Alexander Rae, two men imprisoned on charges of debt, were next to enter the affray and were able to speak with Thomas Morrin. In their testimonies, they both stated that Morrin was on his feet and lucid when he spoke to them. Morrin confirmed that Haggart had inflicted the violent blows to his head. Shortly afterwards, Mrs Hudleston, who lived near the prison, ran to give assistance. In her evidence to the court, she stated that Morrin had told her that Haggart had struck him.

Archibald Blacklock, the surgeon who attended to Morrin's wounds, supplied medical evidence to the court. He detailed that the victim had received five separate injuries to the head, the most pervasive exposing the bone above his left eye. It was decided to seek further medical assistance from

Dr Laing and a consensus was reached to perform a trepanning, which it was hoped would alleviate the most serious injury.[43]

Unfortunately, this medical intervention did not prove successful. Morrin's condition soon deteriorated and he lost consciousness. Later that evening, Thomas Morrin died from his injuries and a post-mortem examination confirmed that he had suffered multiple skull fractures.

As the trial ended, the Solicitor General addressed the jury on behalf of the Crown and informed them that, 'it was not necessary to prove that the mortal blows were given by the prisoner, it was sufficient to prove he was involved.' He detailed to the jury that the victim of this terrible crime had repeatedly confirmed in the final hours of his life that Haggart had inflicted the blows. This was corroborated by the testimony of witnesses who spoke with Thomas Morrin after the attack. In his opinion, it was unfeasible for the jury to consider any verdict other than one of murder.

The defence countered that Simpson's witness testimony could not be relied upon as he was a known criminal. In addition, the witnesses who spoke to Thomas Morrin and heard him implicate Haggart in the aftermath of the attack could not guarantee that the victim was in possession of his senses when he made that claim. Further still, the defence found it disconcerting that the prosecution had not brought Dunbar to the witness stand – after all, he was complicit in planning the escape.

The Crown asserted that Dunbar could not have provided testimony to the case as he had already faced transportation for crimes of which he had been convicted. The defence countered that, without the testimony of Dunbar, it was not possible to carry out a cross-examination. After all, Haggart contended that Dunbar had been the one to strike the fatal blows. Despite the spirited efforts of the defence, the jury did not give any credence to Haggart's assertion and found him guilty without retiring to reach a verdict.

During the sentencing process, the judge did not offer any lenience to the guilty man and Haggart was duly sentenced to death, upon which his body would be conveyed to Dr Alexander Munro, Professor of Anatomy at Edinburgh University, for dissection.

In the weeks before his execution, George Combe visited David Haggart.[44] Through a mixture of dictated views from Haggart and Combe's own personal input, a biography of the prisoner was set to text. It was published as *The Life of David Haggart* and Combe enclosed an appendix, detailing his phrenological notes on Haggart. Although the book appeared to offer a truthful account of David Haggart's life, Lord Cockburn wrote in 1848 that the text was, 'a tissue of absolute lies, not of mistakes, or of exaggerations, or of fancies, but of sheer and intended lies. And they all had one object, to make him appear a greater villain than he really was.' Despite Cockburn's vilification of the book, he made certain mistakes himself, placing Haggart several years older than he really was. In addition, the image of Haggart on the front of the book was never professed to be, 'by his own hand'.

Prior to Haggart's execution he was restricted to a diet of bread and water. Realising that his fate was sealed, the prisoner turned to the Bible for comfort. On the evening before his execution, Haggart only managed a fitful sleep When he took his final steps onto the scaffold, he was composed and beseeched the people in the crowd to avoid, 'the heinous crime of disobedience to one's parents, inattention to the Holy Scriptures, being idle and disorderly and especially Sabbath-breaking'. Thereafter, he said his final prayers for forgiveness and faced the last drop.

Chapter 6

1902: Death Dealer at Surgeons' Hall

❖❖❖

*Surgeons' Hall, Edinburgh.
Image Source: Public Domain.*

Edinburgh has been at the centre of Scottish life for over half a millennium and has witnessed cataclysmic change from the mid-sixteenth century reformation, which established the dominance of the Protestant faith in Scotland and led to eventual regal and political union with England. In addition, the eighteenth-century Scottish Enlightenment recognised Edinburgh as an international mecca for new thinking in subjects such as history, economics, science, philosophy and medicine, represented by the Edinburgh Medical School, established in 1726. Renaissance men such as David Hume, Adam Smith and Lord Monboddo[45] emerged as the leading intellectuals of the day and interpreted changing social patterns.

Yet within this impressive configuration, Edinburgh's Royal College of Surgeons predates all these bodies, originating in 1505 when the Barber Surgeons of Edinburgh were formally incorporated as a craft in the city. Over the centuries the college has evolved to include the teaching of anatomy and surgery, training of surgeons and examination of their acquired knowledge. Headquartered in the magnificent Surgeons' Hall in Edinburgh, the present Category A listed site was designed by the renowned architect William Henry Playfair[46] and completed in 1832. While the primary function of the college has been to champion advances in medical science and improve patient health, some have utilised nefarious methods to fulfil their ambitions, as in any profession.

Cases such as that of Dr Knox[47] and the murderers Burke and Hare[48] are anomalies that affected the wider public, but any institution of antiquity has its own personal losses, which live long in the memory.

The 24th June 1902 began as a special day for Professor William Ivison Macadam.[49] At around quarter to ten in the morning, Ivison Macadam arrived at the laboratory at Surgeons' Hall, resplendent in his uniform as he had intended to lead his battalion's embarkation on a ship which he had chartered for their transportation to the coronation of Edward VII.[50] By eleven o'clock that morning, he was in deep conversation with his brother Stevenson at Surgeons' Hall when Daniel McClinton, a porter, entered the laboratory and, armed with a rifle, promptly fired two shots at Ivison Macadam, killing him almost instantly.

Colonel William Ivison Macadam, Royal Scots Forth VI Brigade 1st Jan 1896.
Image Source: Family photograph. Authority to use William I. Macadam, archives and grandson-Ivison Macadam Archives, Runton Old Hall, Norfolk, UK. Authority to use William I. Macadam, archivist, owner of archive and grandson (kind gift to the archive by the subject's great grandson Robin Bell) Copyright: CC BY-SA 4.0

Turning the weapon on laboratory assistant James Kirkcaldie, he fired yet again. Fortunately, Kirkcaldie was able to crouch behind a desk, avoiding injury. A young student named James Rae Forbes was not so lucky – he entered the laboratory at Surgeons' Hall from the main street and, unaware of what had taken place, was shot twice by McClinton, leaving him mortally wounded. The teenager passed away just a few hours later.

The senseless killings sparked outrage within Edinburgh society and, on 26th June 1902, Ivison Macadam's funeral coffin was given full military honours and ferried on a gun carriage drawn by six horses and riders and a cortege featuring over 1,000 troops.

Rather ghoulishly, the coronation decorations for Edward VII's aborted investiture – which was postponed due to emergency appendicitis – still lined the streets. Yet this did not diminish the funeral procession, as the victim's widow Sarah Macadam and their five children, Myra (22), Elison[51] (20), Barkly (15), Constance (13) and Ivison[52] (7), witnessed a genuine outpouring of grief from the public. Such were the numbers involved that the cortège stretched four miles between the family home ('Slioch', in Edinburgh's Lady Road) to Portobello Cemetery.

Meanwhile, James Rae Forbes was transferred from Edinburgh's Royal Infirmary to the Caledonian Railway Station, escorted by a detachment of the 9th Volunteer Battalion (Highlanders), the Royal Scots. The body was then transported to Stirling Cemetery for burial, also on 26th June 1902. Many locals turned out to pay their respects before the deceased was laid to rest in a private funeral ceremony according to the wishes of his family.

In the months preceding the trial, local and national newspapers carried extensive articles charting the life and career of the analytical chemist Ivison Macadam. He had been educated at Edinburgh's Royal High School and Heidelberg University before following in his father's[53] footsteps in 1873 when he started to lecture in medicine and veterinary science. Two years later Macadam joined the 5th (Leith) Volunteer Battalion of the Royal Scots Guards, and through his endeavours a company of the regiment was established in Portobello, Edinburgh.

Noted as a natural leader of men, Macadam commanded the defence of the Blackford Hill high point in Edinburgh at the end of the Crimean War and during the protracted Anglo-Russia tensions which followed. Rising to the position of Commandant of the battalion, Macadam succeeded Colonel Cranston in 1896 to become Brigade-Major of the Royal Scots Forth Volunteer Infantry and led the battalion at Queen Victoria's Diamond Jubilee in 1897. Macadam was subsequently appointed Colonel-in-Command of the reformed 1st Lothians, and in 1902 became commander of the Second Scottish Volunteer Coronation Battalion for Edward VII's coronation.

Macadam also excelled in his academic career where he proved to be a progressive educator who encouraged women to participate in lectures at the Veterinary College and at Surgeons' Hall, despite women being banned from taking academic degrees at most British universities. Following pioneering women such as Sophia Jex-Blake[54] Macadam established his own medical classes for women at Surgeons' Hall in 1887, and he also taught chemistry at the Edinburgh College of Medicine for Women.[55]

In addition, Macadam had an expansive role as an educator of medical and dental scholars at Surgeons' Hall for the Royal College of Surgeons of Edinburgh and for Edinburgh University. Later in his career, Macadam made the assiduous decision to appoint his daughter Elison to be his assistant. Not only did this make lectures more welcoming to women students, it also demonstrated that it was not just men who were qualified to carry out the work.

Equally adept in charitable endeavours, Macadam was an active member of the Freemason's society, where he was a Grand Master in the movement and in both the Grand Lodge and Depute Grand Principal of the Supreme Grand Royal Arch Chapter of Scotland. After the death of his father in 1901, Macadam made the permanent move to Surgeons' Hall and developed a successful working partnership in the field of analytical chemistry with his younger brother, Stevenson Macadam.

Somewhat overlooked in the tragedy was the second victim, James Rae Forbes, who had been attending classes in analytical chemistry under the tutelage of Macadam with a view to following his father Simon Forbes into the family distillery business. At the time of the murders, Forbes was staying at the family home (Ravenscraig in Mortonhall Road, Edinburgh) while his father oversaw the Peterhead-based Glenugie Distillery. A forward-thinking man, Simon Forbes had taken over the licence in 1884 and over the course of the next thirty years made wholesale improvements and additions to the business. When Simon Forbes died in 1928, aged 82, he had acquired a personal fortune of £43,655 – equivalent to £2.8 million nowadays, taking inflation into account. Despite enjoying a happy marriage, a loving family and business success, he never came to terms with the tragic loss of his son which haunted him for the rest of his life.

When Daniel McClinton (46) of 31A Windsor Street, Edinburgh entered the dock on Thursday 18th September 1902, the charge sheet stated that, on 24th June 1902, he discharged a loaded rifle, killing William Ivison Macadam (46) and James Rae Forbes (18). The defence counsel Mr Wilson advised the court that a special petition had been entered, stating that, in addition to the plea of not guilty to the murder charges, at the time of the crime the accused was insane and labouring under delusions, which compelled him to commit the act.

The first witness to take to the stand was Stevenson Macadam (37), brother of the late Ivison Macadam. He stated that he had employed Daniel McClinton in 1897 and, over the course of the last five years, he had found him to be a willing member of staff in his capacity as an attendant at Surgeons' Hall. On 24th June 1902, Stevenson Macadam arrived at the laboratory at half past nine in the morning and noticed McClinton carrying out his duties as normal.

At eleven o'clock that morning Stevenson Macadam was standing beside his brother in the laboratory when the southwest door opened. Looking round, he noticed McClinton coming into view with his rifle in his hand and an ammunition belt on his shoulder. Stevenson Macadam turned back to his brother as they were in conversation, and did not see the accused walk into the room, but he heard his footsteps. The witness stated that the next thing he was aware of was a shot, then another one, fired in quick succession. He spun around to see Clinton on the other side of the room with his rifle. At that point he did not realise that Ivison had been shot. As far as he could remember, his brother had staggered past him. Stevenson Macadam then crossed the room but McClinton ordered him to stop and said, 'I will not shoot you if you stand where you are. If you interfere with me, I will.'

James Kirkcaldie, the head laboratory assistant, then came into McClinton's field of fire but managed to avoid injury. At this point the bell rang and Stevenson Macadam asked McClinton to go and attend to it, hoping that he might be able to disarm him as he did so. However, McClinton flatly refused and Stevenson Macadam answered the door to James Rae Forbes. As Forbes entered the room, McClinton fired two rounds of ammunition directly at the young student. As

McClinton fired, Stevenson Macadam heard him say, 'this is another of the same lot.' McClinton stated that there were two other men with whom he wanted to get even – Thomas Seaton, the janitor, and William Mitchell, the porter.

Deciding against pursuing them, McClinton walked up to Stevenson Macadam carrying the rifle, which he was about to hand to him. McClinton then noted, 'Mind Steve, it's loaded.' The accused then took back the rifle and emptied the remaining five cartridges out of the magazine on to the floor. Stevenson Macadam secured the rifle from McClinton and rushed over to check on his brother but to no avail, as he was already dead.

Under further questioning, the witness revealed that some sort of ill will existed between McClinton and his brother. McClinton had erroneously formed the opinion that Ivison Macadam was trying to blacken his name. On one occasion, McClinton indicated that Ivison Macadam was using his influence as a Colonel in the first Lothian Volunteer Brigade to make the accused lose his pension. Stevenson Macadam had asked how this could be but McClinton failed to supply any further information.

Next to provide testimony was James Kirkcaldie, who declared that he was the chief assistant in Ivison Macadam's laboratory and had known the accused since 1897. On the morning of 24th June, he witnessed McClinton shoot Professor Macadam and then turn the weapon in his direction. McClinton fired his rifle but the witness was able to scramble to safety. After this, the outer doorbell rang, and Stevenson Macadam answered the door. Young James Rae Forbes then entered proceedings and was shot twice by McClinton. The prosecution counsel made efforts to clarify the mental condition of Daniel McClinton, to which Kirkcaldie replied that, 'the accused was a quiet and morose man but at no time had he suspected McClinton of being insane.'

Lieutenant James Lowdon of Edinburgh City Police clarified McClinton's emotional state further and declared that he appeared to be perfectly rational. On entering the laboratory Lowdon found the accused sitting in the corner with his legs crossed, looking very calm and collected. Only later that evening while McClinton was in his cell did he make a comment to the police, noting that, 'That man had been nagging me and I could not stand it.'

Sir Henry Littlejohn[56] provided medical testimony and described to the court how he had visited McClinton at the police station shortly after his arrest. Littlejohn stated that the accused marched into view in military style. On recognising Littlejohn, he said, 'Oh Dr Litteljohn, I'll swing for this. I don't regret having done it. I am prepared to do it again.' Later that same evening McClinton noted that, 'he had suffered a great deal from them' when the doctor challenged him about the awful business.

Littlejohn took time to conduct fuller interviews with McClinton in the following months and concluded that McClinton was an old military campaigner who presented with no noticeable sign of mental illness. At all times, the clinician found the accused to be fully cognisant with his actions in murdering Ivison Macadam and James Rae Forbes and able to pinpoint details of the day in question. Dr George R. Wilson[57] from Mavisbank Asylum,[58] Loanhead, then provided expert testimony on the mental state of Daniel McClinton.

In Wilson's opinion the prisoner was in good health, his demeanour was orderly and he possessed a sound intellect. McClinton repeatedly stated he had suffered provocation from Macadam and that he found fault with him, often unnecessarily, and conveyed his views in an offensive manner.

As Ivison Macadam had taken against him, McClinton informed Dr Wilson that he had been accosted on the street by men he believed to be in league with Macadam. In further meetings Wilson had with the accused, McClinton broke down in tears and admitted sorrow for what he had done. Dr Wilson concluded by stating that McClinton presented as someone who was, 'inconsistent with a state of real delusional inanity'. However, it was quite consistent with delusional insanity that the prisoner should be able to give a full account of the occurrence immediately after his apprehension.

As the defence case got underway, Alexander Gibb, a veteran of the 71st Regiment, Highland Light Infantry, of which McClinton was also a member, detailed his long friendship with the Lismoine native. Gibb declared that McClinton had confided to him that, on the death of Mr Macadam Snr, his working life had become intolerable as Ivison Macadam was plotting against him. The witness stated that, when he visited the accused prior to the killings, McClinton was unable to keep eye contact and kept counting his fingers, twisting his moustache and scowling. Mary Gibb, wife of the previous witness, went further in her testimony, explaining that a marked change had taken place in McClinton's demeanour and he genuinely believed that people had turned against him. From the way he spoke about his work and people who he believed were watching him, she thought that he was on the brink of insanity.

The most anticipated testimony of the proceedings came from the wife of the accused. Mrs Jessie McClinton stated under oath that she married Daniel McClinton in 1882 and they had enjoyed a happy marriage.

In the previous few years she had become aware of eccentric behaviour in her husband's character. Recounting several events, she outlined that McClinton had grown his beard to disguise himself from those who he believed to be watching him. On another occasion McClinton informed his wife that a policeman had been keeping an eye on him at the behest of Ivison Macadam. On the day of the slayings Mrs Clinton noted that her husband had taken his rifle stating as he left that he would be going for a 'volley firing' after work so would not require an evening meal. Nothing in his character that morning suggested to Mrs McClinton that he was going to carry out such terrible acts.

The defence then called Dr John Batty Tuke[59] to provide further medical opinion of Daniel McClinton's mental state. In his role as Superintendant at Saughton Asylum, Dr Tuke spent over twenty years as a specialist clinician in insanity cases. At the request of the defence, he visited McClinton on 13th September 1902. His findings from that meeting confirmed that, in his professional opinion, Daniel McClinton was suffering from delusional insanity. McClinton talked at length of Ivison Macadam trying to trap him into being dishonest and indicated that the police were constantly watching him, describing them as 'paid degraders'. While the plotting was initially confined to Ivison Macadam, it expanded to include Freemasons.

Dr Tuke quantified his views on McClinton, stating that, in a case of delusional insanity, there need not be any hallucinations. He adhered to his view that McClinton was insane and thus not responsible for his murderous actions. Under cross-examination from the Crown, Dr Tuke further noted that, 'a man who harbours delusions may do so for months yet when they became stronger than his own will, then the sufferer would allow these delusions freedom to play.'

As the two-day trial drew to a close, the closing arguments and summing up of the judge took the best part of the day. In his Charge to the Jury, the judge instructed them as follows: 'Accused persons were always presumed to be sane until the opposite was proved. Accordingly, it was for the defence to establish that the prisoner was suffering, not only from insanity, but from insanity of such a kind and quality that he could not be held morally responsible for his acts, before the defence in the present case could succeed.'

Despite an overwhelming belief in legal circles that there would be a guilty verdict for the two murders, the jury took less than thirty-five minutes to return a verdict of culpable homicide by a majority. Turning to Daniel McClinton, the judge stated, 'The jury have taken a merciful view, and they have found you guilty of culpable homicide.' However, 'culpable homicide is a crime which ranges from cases where there is very little blame to cases which almost reach murder and it cannot be doubted that your case falls into the latter category. My duty therefore is to sentence you to penal servitude for the whole term of your natural life.'

Despite the erroneous sentence of penal servitude Daniel McClinton became a prisoner at H.M. Prison, Peterhead, where, despite being an industrious worker, he was deemed undependable and sly. In the final years of his life, he developed very serious delusional problems and regularly complained, in paranoid delusions, that his food was being poisoned by Ivison Macadam's son, who was a fellow prisoner. McClinton was declared insane in 1921 and removed to the Criminal Lunatic Department at Perth, where he died in July 1923, aged sixty-seven, from peritoneal cancer.

Daniel McClinton. Court artist image 1902.
Source: Newspaper image © The British Library Board. All rights reserved.
With thanks to The British Newspaper Archive (www.britishnewspaperarchive.co.uk).

The case highlights the changing dynamics of the Scottish legal system at the turn of the twentieth century. There was no longer an overriding need for the jury to convict on the charge of murder alone. Indeed, the jury was progressive in offering a verdict of culpable homicide.

The medical opinion documented by Dr Tuke, corroborated by the evidence provided by those closest to McClinton, indicated a man in turmoil, obviously suffering from delusion, which intensified with the passage of time. While this was not a perfect outcome by the standards of the day, the trial punished McClinton for his crimes and gave the families of Ivison Macadam and James Rae Forbes justice. It also highlighted that culpable homicide serves an important role in the Scottish judicial system as it offers two certainties to those convicted on the charge. First, the charge cannot be made unless the accused's behaviour has brought about the death of someone else and second, it is always deemed less serious than murder.

*William Ivison Macadam grave, Portobello Cemetery.
On the 22nd December 1903, a monument in Portobello Cemetery was unveiled by Sir John Halliday, M.D., vice-president of the Royal College of Surgeons, at the Colonel's grave. This with a bronze likeness of Colonel Macadam is in grey stone and was also designed by the colonel's friend W. Grant Stevenson RSA.
Image Source: Public Domain.*

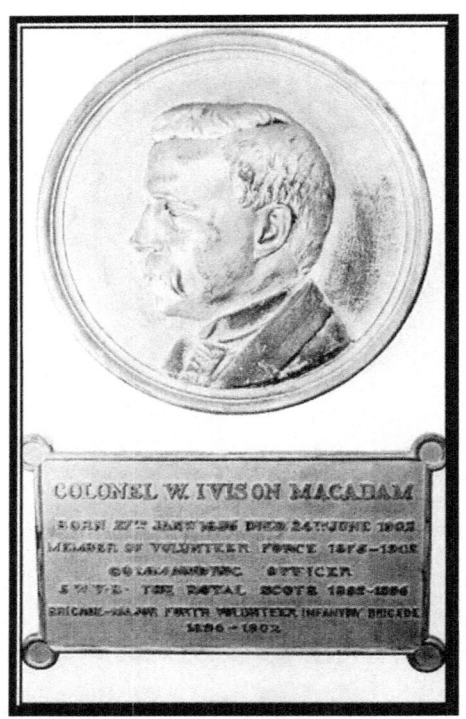

Royal Scots monument to Colonel Macadam, originally situated at Dalmeny Street, Drill Hall, Leith on 21st December 1903. When this was demolished the monument was resituated at Hepburn House Army Reserve Centre, 89 East Claremont Street, Edinburgh.
Image Source: Public Domain.

Chapter 7

1903: A Coachman's Lament

❖❖❖

Duns is a small market town situated in the major agricultural district of Berwickshire, commonly referred to as the 'Merse'. This old Scottish expression references the rich alluvial soils of the pastoral lands between the River Tweed to the south and the uplands of the Lammermuir Hills to the north and west. Despite the town's rich farming heritage, Duns is perhaps more strongly associated with its distinctive role in Scotland's uncompromising history.

Duns was first referenced prior to 1179 when 'Hugo de Duns' acted as a witness to the charter of Roger d'Eu, granting the benefice from the church of Langton to Kelso Abbey under a policy of 'in liberam et perpetuam elemosinam'. Essentially, this charter transferred the revenues of Langton Church to the monks of Kelso in a free and lasting agreement. Circa 1265, noted philosopher John Duns Scotus,[60] one of the most influential theologians–philosophers of the High Middle Ages, was born in the town. Among his most controversial proclamations was that religion was based on faith rather than reason. This highly contentious view led to the word 'dunce' becoming a term utilised to describe an educational under-achiever.

The early settlement was first established on the incline of Duns Law, near the original site of Duns Castle, constructed in 1320 by the Earl of Moray, nephew of Robert the Bruce. However, it was during the invasion of Scotland in 1372 by Henry, Lord Percy, the English March Warden, and his 7,000 troops, that Duns became an integral part of Scottish history. While camped at Duns, the English cavalry horses were alarmed at night by a type of rattle made from dried skins with pebbles inside that the local inhabitants used to scare wild animals and birds away from their livestock and crops.

The encampment awoke in disarray and the English force was routed by the townsmen. The event is commemorated as the Battle of Duns, and is the source of the town's motto, Duns Dings A[61] Despite this success Duns continued to be involved in cross-border wars and, in 1545, Henry VIII's troops destroyed the original town during the 'rough wooings', during the English monarch's ill-fated attempt to persuade the Scots that the young Mary Queen of Scots should enter into a marriage with his son.

During the First Bishops' War[62] in 1639, Duns was of strategic importance to the Covenanters' army, becoming the marshalling point for General Leslie's forces as they prepared to engage with the Crown forces of King Charles I, encamped at Berwick. Despite the opposing forces failing to engage in battle, Leslie took up residence at the castle. Such was the enduring tactical significance of Duns that Oliver Cromwell put a garrison in the town after the Battle of Dunbar in 1650. In 1670, Duns and its surrounding estate were acquired by Sir John Cockburn and, in 1696, the estate was sold to John Hay, first Marquess of Tweeddale.

Not until the relevant peace that followed the final Jacobite rebellion in 1746, however, did Duns begin to settle into the normal rhythms of a prosperous and expanding parish. Such was its success that many of the administrative functions of the county were carried out in the town and in 1903, a parliamentary bill formally recognised Duns as the county town of Berwickshire. Despite this achievement a crime of familicide[63] in the same year rocked the market town to its very core and challenged Edwardian sensibilities.

Lanark Lodge, a well-appointed villa situated at Bridgend on the eastern outskirts of Duns and a little to the east of the railway station, was an affluent abode where life still functioned at a more relaxed pace. The property included a staff of a coachman and gardener. The coachman, John Newbigging, occupied the small two-room gatehouse cottage with his wife Margaret and their four young daughters. On Wednesday 15th April 1903, Mrs McKie, the owner of Lanark Lodge, was absent from her home on a trip to the south of England. The day began as usual with Peter Paterson, the gardener, undertaking his usual duties involving keeping the outside of the property clean and presentable while tending to the lawn and flowerbeds. As the morning progressed, Paterson became concerned that his colleague John Newbigging had not appeared for work. More perplexing, though, was the unbroken stillness of his cottage.

By mid-morning, the children of the house, usually seen playing about, were missed by the neighbours. Paterson became more worried and made several attempts to rouse the house without any reply. Fearing that something was seriously amiss, Paterson hurried to inform John Newbigging's father, who promptly dispatched his younger son Thomas to attend the house. Thomas Newbigging made similar efforts to obtain admission to the cottage. On failing to do so, he accessed the property by a rear window. Within seconds, the neighbours gathered outside the property heard a piercing shriek. Thomas sobbed, 'They are all dead!'

The catastrophic events were quickly reported to the local police and Sergeant Young and Constable Brand attended the scene with Dr Mackenzie in his role as acting Medical Officer of Health. Such was the magnitude of the murder scene that the Procurator Fiscal, Mr W.B. MacQueen, and Sheriff Dundas were also in attendance. The sight that met the public authorities was distressing in the extreme. In the kitchen of the house there were two beds. In one of these beds were two of the young girls. The body of a third child was in the other bed, while the body of the eldest girl, which appeared to have fallen from the bed, lay on the floor in front of it.

The body of Margaret Newbigging and her husband lay behind the door leading to the hallway. In each case, death resulted from a laceration to the throat. Dr Mackenzie asserted that the three youngest children had died while sleeping but the oldest girl, Maggie, and her mother had fought valiantly for their lives. A blood-soaked open razor, which had dropped from the hand of John Newbigging, was found on the floor beside his corpse. The bodies were already showing signs of rigor mortis, leading Dr Mackenzie to conclude that death must have occurred at or around daybreak.

Contemplating this tragedy, it is salient to outline the life that John Newbigging shared with his family. Viewed by all who knew him as a diligent, hardworking and even-tempered man, John was born in Duns in 1871. His wife, Margaret White, daughter of Mr William White, a school board officer, was born in Eyemouth in 1871. The couple married in 1896 and, over the course of their seven-year marriage, they were blessed with four daughters – Maggie 5, Mary, 4, Jane, 2, and Helen, also known as 'Lilly', who was less than a year old. In the days before the tragedy, Mrs Newbigging had returned from a trip with the children to visit her father in Eyemouth. She was distressed to find that her husband had been suffering from frequent bouts of insomnia in her absence for which he had not sought any medical treatment.

At his wife's behest, John Newbigging called in Dr Mackenzie on Monday 13th April, who promptly prescribed bromide of potassium to alleviate his condition. On visiting the following day, Mrs Newbigging informed Dr Mackenzie that her husband had slept well the previous evening. Although the doctor was gratified to hear this, he asked John Newbigging's friends to keep a watchful eye on him as the prolonged effects of insomnia could include mental derangement. Later that evening, John enjoyed a visit from his father, who found his son to be cheerful and content in the company of his wife and children. With his son's acquiescence, Robert Newbigging obtained another bromide powder from the doctor, which the patient duly took and went to bed.

From this point we enter the realm of conjecture, although the considered medical opinion of the day was that John Newbigging was momentarily overtaken by a form of homicidal mania, which compelled him to kill his family. It was asserted that Newbigging had risen from his bed, partially dressed, and begun to light the fire in the grate to help his wife prepare for the chores of the day. At this point the murderous intent had taken hold and he carried out this terrible act.

In such trying times, the task of making ready the bodies for burial was given to Nurse Bardsley, daughter of the Bishop of Carlisle and a highly respected member of the community known for tending to the needs of the sick and infirm. Despite receiving offers of assistance from many local women, Nurse Bardsley realised that it would be far too traumatic an experience for those unaccustomed to death, let alone such a harrowing situation. If needs be, she could access the services of Sergeant Young from the local police force and John Leslie, the district's sanitary officer.

When the 'chesting'[64] of the bodies took place at the undertaker's parlour, Robert Newbigging was in attendance, although Margaret's father was too distressed to be there. Three coffins were presented to the family – the first contained Maggie and Mary, while another belonged to Margaret Newbigging and her baby girl Lilly. Jane and John Newbigging occupied the final casket. The funeral service for the Newbigging family took place on Saturday 18th April 1903 at the small cottage where the family had lived. The Rev. W.D. Herald, minister of Duns, gave a moving oration to the immediate family who had gathered. The early hour was chosen to avoid crowds of onlookers and the subsequent funeral cortege to the cemetery was conducted with solemnity.

At the beginning of the twentieth century, homicidal mania and its associated brethren overtook conditions such as epilepsy, insanity and brain injuries to rank second only to melancholia and delusion as the most cited medical testimony to support a diagnosis of extreme mental impairment. In the Edwardian era, medical consensus dictated that homicidal mania had an overriding imperative, namely murder. A person suffering such an event would experience intense delusions from which they could not draw away, in the most acute cases leading to murder. As death offered the only chance of relief, according to the insane reasoning of the sufferer, they believed that their family should also die.

However, this form of diagnosis does not sit well with this case and there is a lack of evidence to formulate a definitive conclusion. John Newbigging arguably enjoyed a very loving marriage – his children were healthy and happy, he was respected and valued by his employer and he had no overriding financial concerns. Considered medical opinion would now classify John Newbigging as having carried out an act of 'familicide'.

In most cases of this, the adult male of the family kills his children and very often his partner too. Clinical psychology notes two specific categories of familicide – in the former, the children are murdered and the killer commits suicide. This is normally associated with a bitter separation and the action of the killer is to make the surviving spouse suffer perpetual feelings of loss and guilt. However, John Newbigging falls into the latter category, perhaps through some ill-founded belief that he would not be able to support his family. It was noted at the time by members of his immediate family that he might have erroneously thought that his job was in jeopardy and, with it, his home. Potassium of bromide was used as a pharmacological sleep aid to exert an anaemic action on his brain, yet this had extraordinarily little time to have a therapeutic impact. The depression that John Newbigging felt may have developed over the course of his transition from acute to chronic insomnia. With such fears upon him and in his altered state of mind, he took the only course of action he believed was available to him.

Artist's drawing of the cottage where the Newbigging tragedy took place, 1903.
Image Source: Newspaper image © The British Library Board. All rights reserved. With thanks to The British Newspaper Archive (www.britishnewspaperarchive.co.uk).

Chapter 8

1923: Mercy Neither Given nor Received

❖❖❖

The last woman hanged in Scotland presents a most perplexing and genuinely macabre killing. Born in the picturesque town of Oban in Argyll and Bute in 1893, Susan McAllister experienced an impoverished childhood. Although Oban enjoyed something of a renaissance within Victorian society as a holiday spot following the advent of the railway, which greatly improved the transportation network, the area was beset with financial difficulties. The ill-fated Oban Hydro and McCaig's Tower,[65] an eye-catching local landmark the construction of which aimed to give work to local stonemasons, all fell by the wayside as financial ineptitude and sheer bad luck struck the town.

In these circumstances, Susan made the decision at an early age to seek a better life. Through a variety of low paid work she managed to save enough money to make the move to Glasgow at the age of seventeen. Unfortunately, the bright lights of the big city offered only more of the same and Susan found herself struggling financially. In 1914 she met and married John McLeod, a twenty-four-year-old from the island of Lewis. This should have been a happy time in the lives of the young couple but Susan found herself pregnant and alone as her husband enlisted in the British Army and was sent overseas at the outbreak of the First World War.

That year, Susan gave birth to a baby girl named Janet. However, when the baby was only a few months old, news came to Susan that her husband had been killed on active service in the trenches of northern France. At this point, it is exceedingly difficult to discern what became of Susan and her daughter – in the intervening seven years, there is no official record of either. We take up the case in 1922 with Susan married to John Newell. For the first time she had found an enduring relationship, happiness and a decent stepfather for Janet. As was the story throughout Susan's life, her happiness was short lived.

At Christmas 1922, John Newell lost his job at British Tube Works, Coatbridge. Over the course of the next six months, the relationship between the couple soured. Newell was unable to find employment and Susan once again faced interminable financial hardship.

Under these circumstances, the first documented evidence of Susan's volatile nature emerges. The couple lived in the village of Summerlee, Lanarkshire, following their marriage and it was decided that the family would decamp to lodgings at 2 Newlands Street, Coatbridge. On 19th June 1923, the relationship between Susan and John exploded in acrimony, fuelled by alcohol. Not for the first time, Susan violently attacked her husband in a fit of rage. Such was the effect on John Newell that he reported the attack to the local police but they did not intercede because of lack of evidence and a genuine unwillingness on their part to get involved in domestic disputes. Deciding that the breakdown of the marriage was irreversible, John Newell left his wife and young Janet. Sensing further trouble, the landlady of

Newlands Street, Mrs Young, gave Susan Newell notice to quit.

The next day, 20th June 1923, was something of a red-letter occasion in the area as the Old Monklands Agriculture Show was due to take place. This was not simply a trade fair to exhibit animals and equipment in competition, but very much a public event, which included shows and attractions for the public to enjoy. For thirteen-year-old street newsvendor John Johnson, there was no time to enjoy the fair. He was an industrious young lad and decided to maximise his sales revenue by selling papers at the fair.

Conscientious in his work, he found himself in Newlands Street later than usual, with newspapers in hand ready to sell to his regular customers. At around quarter to seven in the evening, John knocked on the door of 2 Newlands Street and was readily admitted to the property by Mrs Young, who bought her usual paper. Deciding to knock on the rooms of Mrs Newell, he was invited into the room and Susan took a paper from the young newsvendor.

However, she was unwilling or unable to pay for the paper and an argument broke out between Susan and John. It is not known if what followed resulted from the vicious temper of Susan Newell alone or was combined with the effects of alcohol, but the mother strangled the boy instantaneously.

John Johnson, murder victim of Susan Newell.
Image Source: With thanks to The British Newspaper Archive.

At around eight o'clock in the evening, Janet returned home from playing and was confronted with the harrowing sight of the murdered boy. For a seven-year-old child, the magnitude of what she saw must have been impossible to grasp. Sworn to secrecy by her mother, Janet was forced to help Susan wrap the body of John Johnson in a rug. The following morning Susan undertook the task of disposing of the body and at around eight o'clock in the morning, she was seen pulling a child's go-cart, which appeared to be heavily laden with clothes. At around half past nine, at a junction in Bargeddie, Susan asked a delivery driver named Thomas Dickson if he could offer her and Janet a lift into Glasgow as they were looking for new accommodation.

About thirty minutes later, the truck pulled up at Parkhead forge in the east end of Glasgow. Dickson began to lower the go-cart down to Susan, who was waiting in the street, but the sheer weight was too much for the slightly built woman to manage. Dickson was able to catch the go-cart but the bundle had become dislodged and John Johnson's head suddenly appeared, his foot jutting out at the bottom of the cart. With deathly calm, Susan Newell covered up the body and walked away.

A vigilant citizen witnessed the entirety of this brief exchange and decided to follow Newell. As the resident shadowed Newell, she met up with her sister on Duke Street and told her of the horrific scene she had witnessed. Newell continued along the road and then moved into an access lane beside Number 630. Deciding that the authorities needed to be informed, one sister continued to watch the tenement while the other set out to inform the police.

A local resident named Robert Foot was exiting a local newsagents shop when one of the women cried out, 'There is a woman away up that entry way and she is carrying a dead body.' Hastened by the terrible news, Foot decided to follow Newell who, by this time, had realised that she had entered the back court of a block of tenement flats with no other means of exit. Panicked, Newell discarded her daughter and the go-cart and attempted to climb the back wall to freedom. Fortunately, Constable McGennet entered the affray and intervened, formally arresting Susan Newell.

Number 630 Duke Street was soon awash with the information that a sinister occurrence had taken place. The warren-like nature of tenement buildings meant that a large group of people was soon in attendance, along with the media. The crowd numbers were such that the police had considerable difficulty in accessing the scene. Newell was taken into custody, Janet was recovered to the authorities and the body of John Johnson was removed from the scene. When Newell was questioned at the Eastern Police Station on Tobago Road, she formally implicated her husband as the murderer of the boy. Thoroughly primed for the situation, Janet did as her mother had instructed her and corroborated her story.

The post-mortem examination of John Johnson was caried out by the eminent Professor John Glaister[66] with the assistance of Dr John Anderson, the pathologist at the city's Victoria Infirmary. The findings confirmed that the cause of death was manual strangulation and that recent burning had occurred to the sides of the head and the scalp. Aware that their prime suspect had fled the police utilising the power of the press, a full description of the wanted man was printed on the front cover of all the major newspapers in Scotland.

As a result, John Newell walked into Haddington Police Station on Friday 22nd of June 1923 and gave himself up to the authorities. It was discovered that Newell had arrived in Haddington the previous evening and informed his landlady that he was seeking labouring work on a farm. Susan Newell was formally remanded into custody and sent to Duke Street Prison, while her estranged husband was transported back to Glasgow.

*Susan & John Newell in the dock 18th September 1923.
Image Source: Newspaper image © The British Library Board.
All rights reserved. With thanks to The British Newspaper Archive
(www.britishnewspaperarchive.co.uk).*

When the case against Susan and John Newell began at the Justiciary Buildings in Glasgow on 18th September 1923, the indictment stated that the married couple murdered John Johnson on 20th June 1923 by beating him on the head with a blunt instrument, throttling him and dislocating the spinal column in his neck. The defendants denied the charge and a special plea of an alibi was lodged on behalf of John Newell, while a petition of insanity was made for Mrs Newell.

Appearing before Lord Alness, the Lord Justice Clerk[67] was Robert Johnson, the father of the murdered boy, who stated that on the evening of his son's disappearance he had gone out to search for him when he had failed to return from the cinema. When he failed to trace John, he contacted the police to report him missing. Mr Johnson recounted that he was at work the following day when the police arrived to take him to the Eastern Police Station to formally identify the body of his son. His wife Margaret corroborated his testimony, collapsing in the courtroom from raw emotion. The most startling evidence to be presented to the court came from young Janet McLeod (8) who stated that she had been out playing with friends and returned home in the evening to find her mother there with the boy. Janet had then gone were her mother to the local public house where Susan Newell had purchased beer, wine and whisky.

Janet further noted that, on returning home, she had seen the body face down on the couch and had gone over to check if he was dead. Further questioning from the prosecution counsel led Janet to confirm that the initial story she had told the policewomen was untrue. Her mother had told her to inform the police that her father, John Newell, had carried out the killing.

As the trial moved into its second day, Detective Sergeant Charles Lockhart detailed that he had travelled to Haddington to return the accused, John Newell, to custody. Lockhart stated that Newell said, 'I know nothing whatever about it.' On returning to Coatbridge John Newell made a voluntary statement that on 20th June 1923 that he was in the Olympia Theatre, Bridgeton Cross, Glasgow, from around seven until nine in the evening. He was in the bar of the establishment on two separate occasion and distinctly remembered the barman telling him that he had overcharged him by mistake.

The medical evidence supplied by Professor Glaister and Dr Anderson concluded that John Johnson was throttled to death in conjunction with a dislocation of the spinal column of his neck. The marks discovered on the deep tissues of the scalp were produced by repeated forcible blows from a blunt instrument, while the burn marks on the left side of his head were concurrent with coming into contact with fire while he was still alive, as shown by the blistering.

The Crown case then rested and John Newell took to the witness box. In his testimony, he declared that he had not run away, knew nothing of the crime and was entirely innocent. It was revealed to the court that Newell was a native of Coatbridge and had married his co-accused in July 1922. During the First World War, he had seen action in France but was discharged on account of wounds that he received in 1915. He recounted the evidence supplied by the police concerning his movements and categorically denied having any involvement in the death of the boy.

Lord Alness was incensed by the shoddy work of the prosecution brief in bringing a charge against John Newell. As a result, John Newell was discharged from the court – a free man.

Lord Kinross took little time – less than fifteen minutes – in presenting the case for the Crown against Mrs Newell. The defence brief Mr Gentles was faced with critical deposition supplied by Dr G. Garry, the medical officer at Duke Street Prison, who stated that he had observed Mrs Newell since she had been admitted to prison in June. Over the course of those months he found her to be, 'intelligent and capable of understanding her position, the charge against her and all the different details'. At all times, Mrs Newell had given a 'clear and fairly satisfactory account of her conduct both before and after the crime'. As far as his observation had revealed, Dr Garry found, 'nothing to satisfy him that Mrs Newell was insane or insane at the time of the crime'.

The defence case continued to focus on the mental condition of their client, stating that if Mrs Newell had killed John Johnston for the sake of a few coppers then the motive of the crime was completely irrational and gave rise to the question of insanity or, at any rate, a complete loss of mental balance. Mr Gentles went on to document the circumstances in which Susan Newell found herself, with little or no money, a husband who had deserted her and faced with the prospect of being made homeless with a young child completely dependent on her. For the briefest of moments, spectators in the court noted that Susan Newell appeared to show her first sign of genuine emotion during the proceedings as tears welled in her eyes, yet almost immediately she regained her passive countenance.

In his summation, Lord Alness put four key questions to the jury. Was John Johnson killed by a person or persons? If so, has Mrs Newell been proven to be the assailant? If she can be so proved, was she sane at the time when she killed the boy? If she was sane at the time, what was the nature of her act – was it murder or culpable homicide?

Lord Alness concluded, 'You are concerned not with mercy but with justice. Merciful considerations reside elsewhere. I am quite sure you will conscientiously and faithfully, and in accordance with the oath you have taken, discharge the duty laid on you.'

It took the jury thirty-five minutes to return a majority verdict of guilty against Susan Newell with a strong recommendation to mercy. Lord Alness pronounced a sentence of death and said that the jury's request for mercy would be forwarded to the proper quarter, and dealt with there. In accordance with the rules of the court, he donned the black cap and passed a sentence of death on Newell, who stared unflinchingly at him as he made his proclamation. The call for mercy was deeply felt throughout Scotland despite the enormity of the crime. No woman had faced the gallows in Scotland for fifty years and in prison reforming circles there was a genuine belief that Newell might be afforded leniency.

Despite concerted efforts to mitigate Newell's sentence, this was not forthcoming and, on 10th October 1923, Susan Newell faced hangman John Ellis. Unfortunately, what should have been a swift process was blighted by Ellis's mistakes. He failed to secure the prisoner's arms after fitting a belt around her waist, incorporating straps to tie her elbows to her body. Newell stepped onto the trapdoor of the gallows; her legs were bound together and the noose was placed around her neck and drawn tight. While the death hood was placed onto her head, the prisoner managed to wriggle free her arm, throw it off and seethe, 'Don't put that thing on me.'

Fearing a similar disordered outcome to that of the recently hanged Edith Thompson,[68] Ellis hastily pulled the trapdoor open and Newell fell to her death, thrashing about wildly as the shocked officials stood on. Such was the effect of the Thompson and Newell hangings on John Ellis that he resigned, living a tortured existence until he finally committed suicide, cutting his own throat with an open razor in full view of his family.

The case of Susan Newell raised unflattering questions about the morality of 1920's Britain. First and foremost, with the burden of proof put forward in the trial, there is little doubt that finding the defendant guilty of the charge of murder was right and proper. Justice for the terrible murder of John Johnson – the primary victim in this trial – was served, a fact that should never be forgotten. However, Susan Newell was also a victim – of the circumstances and of her gender.

Life since the end of the First World War altered perceptions of a woman's role in society. In certain circumstances the male-dominated society would afford a woman leeway but not if they acted against their perceived role in life as a nurturing mother figure. Susan Newell behaved in a manner so unnatural to her gender that she subverted what was considered as the feminine ideal. This is not an example of mitigation, rather it provides an insight into how a woman was treated by the Scottish legal system nearly one hundred years ago. Things were changing from a legal standpoint but the court system could still not reconcile how to deal with a female child killer.

Equally, there was the socio-economic dynamic to consider. It was only five years since women over the age of thirty had been given the right to vote and to do so they needed to be householders, the spouse of a householder, occupiers of a property with an annual rent of £5 and graduates of British universities. Susan Newell did not come from this type of privileged background; she was a simple working-class Scottish woman born into poverty. Would a Scottish court have shown mitigation for a middle-class woman facing the same murder charge? Going by the English court verdict of the Edith Thomson trial the answer would be no. However, Scots law is a hybrid legal system which diverges from its English counterpart as set out in the 1707 Acts of Union. It formally stipulated that, 'no alteration be made in laws which concern private right except for evident utility of the subjects within Scotland.' Therefore large areas of Scots law remain distinct as does its judicial system. Perhaps the question of social hierarchy may have been significant to the verdict of a Scottish court if Susan Newell had originated from the privileged classes.

Of the thirty-four people hanged in Scotland for murder during the 20th century, Susan Newell was the only woman. Prior to her execution the last woman to be hung in Scotland was the notorious baby farmer Jesse King who was executed in Edinburgh in 1889.[69] Ultimately the imponderable remains. Was Susan Newell's actions in killing John Johnson a mental aberration – a brief act of insanity – or was it an act of alcohol-fuelled rage? We shall never know and history will simply record Susan Newell as the last woman to hang in Scotland.

Chapter 9

1927: The Agnes Arbuckle Mystery

❖ ❖ ❖

Glasgow in 1927 was a city in flux. As in the rest of the country, there was a malaise after the General Strike[70] the year before. Working-class families were struggling on the breadline and jobs and opportunities for people to improve their daily lives were scarce. As the effects of the depression spread into every facet of daily life, Glasgow lost much of its heavy industry and a more sinister reputation emerged for the city in the inter-war years, which the city has never been able to fully shake off.

However, the emergence of a gang culture in 1920's Glasgow should not have surprised the ruling establishment. After all, a significant sectarian divide had existed in the city since the 1880s, influenced by the influx of migrants from the Scottish Highlands and Ireland attracted by employment opportunities. With high-density populations of Catholics and Protestants, strong territorial loyalties were established, fostering genuine fears that Glasgow was becoming a city that was ungovernable.

The fictional novel *No Mean City*[71] only exacerbated the situation. The narrative involves an unemployed baker who detailed the minutia of everyday life in the Gorbals area of the city in the 1920's. Not only did the book offer a stark representation of unemployment, ruined lives and a street culture of criminality, it challenged middle-class perceptions and attitudes.

For George Geddes[72] of the Royal Humane Society[73] and George Bissett, a joiner to trade, thoughts of such criminality were a world away as they rowed up the River Clyde early on the morning of Saturday 15th October 1927. At around eight o'clock in the morning the men's attention was drawn to what appeared to be a bundle of clothing partially submerged in the water close to the Glasgow Green bank of the river, about one 150 yards above King's Bridge on Govan Street.

Deciding to investigate further, Geddes stepped into the mud and swung the parcel, which was far heavier than he had expected, on to his boat. On opening the bundle Geddes was horrified to discover a woman's head, which had been wrapped in brown paper. Accompanying the head were several other neatly wrapped packages containing an arm and two legs, which had been sliced off below the knee. The victim's flesh bore severe burns and the woman's ring finger had been sliced off. It was later found tucked away in the folds of brown paper.

Recovering from his initial shock, Geddes contacted Glasgow's Central Police Office[74] and senior officers from the Criminal Investigation Department were dispatched to the scene. Taking charge of the investigation was Superintendent Forbes, a methodical detective who quickly mobilised a squad of over fifty officers to canvas the local community and businesses.

Aside from the grisly discovery, the police had scant evidence to work with and decided to instigate a search of houses throughout the eastern, central and southern districts of the city to recover the torso of the body.

Professor Glaister[75] of Glasgow University was requested to make an initial examination of the human remains and established that the victim was an old woman with sandy brown hair with grey flecks. The victim's hair had been singed at the back of the neck, indicating that the killer had attempted to dispose of the head in a fire. Six distinct wounds were apparent on the head, which appeared to have been inflicted by an axe, while the mouth, nose and cheeks were severely damaged. Professor Glaister concluded in his preliminary findings that the killer had no knowledge of human anatomy.

The difficulty in identifying the murder victim was formidable. Fortunately for the authorities, over the course of the following day, the investigation took a swift and decisive turn. On returning from holiday, Mrs McKay was perturbed to find no trace of her mother-in-law at her home and attended the Central Police Station immediately to report her concerns. After being shown the human remains recovered the day before, Mrs McKay duly identified them as those of her mother-in-law, Mrs Agnes Arbuckle.

Detectives were dispatched immediately to Mrs Arbuckle's home at 213 Main Street on the south side of the city. Unable to gain entrance to the property, the officers visited Mrs Arbuckle's son, James McKay, the husband of the informant, who lived close by at 241 Thistle Street. The police were unsatisfied with McKay's cursory answers to their questions and he was asked to return with the police to his mother's home to allow them access to the premises.

After a painstaking search of the property, the torso was discovered severed and half hidden under a layer of coal and dross in the coal bunker. As a result, James McKay was taken into custody and charged with killing his mother.

As news of the arrest circulated around Glasgow, it emerged that Agnes Arbuckle was a sixty-nine-year-old widow and a woman of temperate habits, who had lived in her home for nearly twenty years. Agnes had suffered terrible loss in the years before her death. One of her sons was reported missing in action during the First World War and another son had passed away more recently. Police established that Agnes called at the local post office to collect a pension in respect of the son who was killed in the war. Neighbours of the victim stated that several weeks had passed since Agnes was last seen – on the day in question, it was believed that she had left to visit the post office as usual but failed to return.

On 12th December 1927, the trial of James McKay (40) got underway at Glasgow High Court. He was charged with killing his mother Agnes Arbuckle (69) on the morning of 28th September 1927. The case for the Crown was led by Mr J.M. Hunter, Advocate Depute, and Mr T.B. Simpson, while the defence case was represented by Mr McDonald KC[76] and Mr John Cameron. A special defence was lodged before Lord Ormidale,[77] the presiding judge. Without prejudice to James McKay's plea of not guilty, a further addendum stated that, during the period libelled, when it was asserted that the defendant committed the crime, the prisoner was insane or in such a state of mental weakness that he was not responsible for his actions.

Among the first testimonies was that of Detective Lieutenant Stirton of the Criminal Investigation Department, who revealed that, when the human remains were located, the accused's demeanour was calm and collected. Stirton concluded by noting that McKay made a voluntary statement to the authorities that his mother had been dead for some ten days and that he had disposed of the body in the Clyde while the torso was deposited in the coal bunker.

Professor Glaister was called next to give his medical findings from the autopsy of Agnes Arbuckle. The clinician detailed that the level of decomposition in the body indicated that Agnes had been dead for between ten and fourteen days before her body was discovered. Professor Glaister stated that the instrument used to inflict the wounds and amputations was a fine-toothed saw. The cause of death was attributed to the multiple wounds, which would have occasioned very severe haemorrhage and trauma-induced shock. The body also showed evidence of blistering concurrent with having been burned although he could not ascertain if this occurred before or after death.

Dr John Anderson, pathologist at the Victoria Infirmary, Glasgow, provided further medical testimony, corroborating the findings of Professor Glaister. Dr Anderson expressed the belief that the wounds inflicted on the face of Mrs Arbuckle occurred while she was still alive, based on the sharp-edged and clear-cut pattern of the wounds. He admitted to the proceedings that, if the scorch marks found on the body had happened while Mrs Arbuckle was alive, they would have been sufficient to have caused death. In a deviation from his previous medical testimony Dr Anderson concluded that the scorch marks were, in his opinion, inflicted when the victim was dead because of the locus of the burns, which were not grouped together. Perhaps the most telling aspect of the trial concerned the mental state of James McKay, which was correlated to his defence plea. Dr David Henderson established that the accused was lucid and provided a full account of his life, including his time as a prisoner during the First World War in the salt mines of Germany.

The witness stated that, in his professional opinion, 'McKay was normal in attitude and manner and understood the charge proffered against him.' There was no evidence of mental delusions and, if the prisoner was in a melancholic state, this was a result of the circumstances in which he found himself.

During their interview, it was revealed that the prisoner was an alcoholic, exacerbated, in McKay's opinion, by his wife living apart from him from March to October and the added responsibility of having to look after their children. Over the course of these months, McKay got into financial difficulties and became reliant on his mother to pay the rent on his home. Unfortunately, he squandered this on alcohol, leading led to an argument. Dr Galbraith of the Central Police was called to provide a second medical opinion on John McKay's mental state. While the accused appeared to be somewhat depressed, Dr Galbraith stated that McKay, 'was amiable in conversation and responded to questioning'. In Galbraith's opinion, there was no evidence to suggest that the prisoner was mentally impaired.

No witnesses were called on behalf of the defence and the case against James McKay very rapidly entered the closing arguments. Addressing the jury, the Advocate Depute Mr J.M. Hunter argued that the case hinged on the plea of insanity. He stated that the contention by the defence that the wounds on the head and neck of Mrs Arbuckle were inflicted after death was quite untenable. The motivation behind the crime was simple – the accused desperately needed money. Mrs Arbuckle had personal savings and the defendant had taken out a life insurance policy on his mother, which meant that the victim's death would benefit him by some £100. Most tellingly of all, James McKay had documents on his person that proved he was practising forging his mother's signature.

Further, the consensus of the medical professionals who interviewed the accused was that he was perfectly rational and displayed no symptoms or manifestations of mental illness. He submitted that Mrs Arbuckle had died from the injuries inflicted by the accused and that he then cut her up in cold blood. The Advocate Depute admitted that the jury had no choice but to return a verdict of guilty on the charge of murder.

Defence counsel Mr James McDonald, KC, began his summation by criticising the Crown case, which stressed a capital charge based on the argument that the death of Mrs Arbuckle resulted from violence inflicted by his client with the intention of causing death. He submitted that this assertion had not been proven. Turning to James McKay's war record, he emphasised that the defendant was, until very recently, a steady and sober man, before a sudden change occurred in his character. Mrs Arbuckle's death was a complete mystery and the jury had to treat it as a case of sudden natural death. Painting a proactive scenario Mr McDonald suggested that an inebriated McKay had visited his mother and found her dead. In this drunken state he had not known what to do and became so alarmed that he decided to conceal the body. As such the verdict should be one of not guilty or not proven, or, in the event of a guilty verdict, the sentence should be a conviction of culpable homicide.

Lord Ormidale stated that the evidence showed that the 'case did not appear to present many difficulties.' The medical assessment was unanimous and stated that death was, 'indicative of the victim having been alive when the injuries were inflicted'. Accordingly, the victim was or might have been a subject of murder. Regarding the plea of insanity, Lord Ormidale highlighted the war record of James McKay, which did him great credit but at no time showed evidence of an altered mental state. As the jury of nine men and six women retired to consider their verdict, an impassive expression remained on the face of James McKay, which did not alter throughout the course of the three-day trial. In less than twenty-five minutes the jury returned a unanimous verdict of guilty.

Lord Ormidale did not prevaricate and judicially passed a sentence of death. He pronounced that James McKay would be conveyed to Duke Street Prison, Glasgow, and hanged there on 4th January 1928 between the hours of eight and ten o'clock in the morning. As he was escorted from the court, McKay turned to his wife and cried 'Cheer up!'

This case represented a turning point in the Scottish legal system as James McKay was the first convicted killer to appeal the court's decision under the terms of the Criminal Appeal (Scotland) Act 1926.[78] The petition proved unsuccessful and on 29th December 1927 James McKay discovered that his sentence would stand. As Sir John Gilmour, Secretary of State for Scotland, noted, 'He was unable to discover sufficient grounds to justify him in advising His Majesty to interfere with the due course of the law.' Less than a month later, James McKay was executed at eight o'clock in the morning on 24th January 1928, having failed to venture any further details on the murder.

James McKay presented as an ambivalent figure throughout his trial and it was notable at the time that he never really demonstrated any remorse for his terrible actions. The defence argument that their client had found his mother dead while he was in a drunken state and disposed of her body had no ring of truth about it whatsoever. Agnes Arbuckle suffered an ignominious end to her life with catastrophic injuries to her face and head, which was severed at the neck. Further, her body was dismembered and the gruesome package in the River Clyde contained a left arm, a thigh, two legs, which had been amputated below the knee, and the victim's ring finger.

The charred area at the back of the victim's neck indicated that the killer either attempted to burn Agnes Arbuckle while disposing of the body or that she had fallen into the fireplace during the attack. What is clear is that McKay was calm, ordered and methodical in disposing of his mother's body, but the killing itself displays all the hallmarks of a frenzied attack. The question remains whether James McKay was suffering from an altered state of mental health.

Traditional thinking first advanced by Sigmund Freud would argue that matricide served as a displacement defence against incestuous impulse. While this has been a proven theory in many such cases, it does not fit neatly with the facts presented in this case. It is far more feasible that James McKay was arguing with his mother over his need for money and her unwillingness to continually bail him out, enraging him and leading to murder. It is known that James McKay had an alcohol dependency problem, was in financial difficulties and, during the First World War, was a prisoner of war in Germany. Did the perpetrator's mental health condition suffer because of these multiple issues to such a degree that he carried out this heinous murder.

A modern interpretation of matricide offers an opinion that goes some way to answering questions about James' McKay's actions. Notable criminology professor Dr Kathleen Heide[79] suggests in her book *Understanding Parricide* that, 'men who commit matricide often reported feeling that their mothers were either ambivalent toward them or excessively domineering. These men were frequently described as considering the act of killing their mothers to maintain their masculinity or as protection against extreme emotions triggered by their mothers' behaviour.'

Duke Street Prison, Glasgow. Executions were carried out at the prison from 1865-1928.
Susan Newell executed here January 23rd, 1923.
John McKay executed here on January 24th, 1927.
Wendy Wood, a Scottish Nationalist political activist who ended up as a prisoner at Duke Street, protested the terrible conditions which women faced while incarcerated. This was instrumental in leading to the decision to close the prison in 1955. It was demolished in 1958.
Image Source: Public Domain.

Chapter 10

1977: What the Butler did Next

❖ ❖ ❖

Left: Archibald Hall aka Roy Fontaine.
Right: Michael Kitto.
Image Source: Wikipedia, Fair use.

In the inter-war years, Glasgow was caught in a paradox between its illustrious past when it was known in the nineteenth century as the second city of the British Empire, renowned as a pre-eminent centre for shipbuilding, and the sectarian metropolis of the 1920's when the police and razor gangs[80] contested ownership of the streets. Despite the deprivation existing in Glasgow when Archibald Thompson Hall was born on 17th June 1924, his father was gainfully employed in the city's main post office in George Square while his mother Marion worked as a waitress at the cosmopolitan Malmaison restaurant in the Central Hotel.

During Hall's formative years, the family moved from the Partick area of the city to Maclean Street in Govan. Situated on the southern outskirts of Glasgow, close to Rangers Football Club, the local people were fortunate to enjoy high levels of employment in the shipyards. Not only did this guarantee regular work, but it was also a skilled industry that ensured a fair day's pay. Growing up in a secure family environment, Hall developed a particularly close relationship with his mother, who always encouraged her son to strive to better himself in life. Unfortunately, Archibald Hall was not predisposed to hard work and, from a young age, he sought to cut corners to fulfil his lofty ambitions.

Hall never quite fitted in with his peers and, throughout his formative years, he maintained no close friendships but developed a fascination with a fantasy lifestyle. He was enamoured with the films of the silver screen and the writings of purported warlock Alister Crowley[81] and his debauched religion, known as 'Thelema'.

By the outbreak of the Second World War, the Hall family had left Scotland for a new home at Catterick Barracks in Yorkshire, where Archibald Snr was employed as a telegraph operator. This was not the only sea change that had taken place – an adopted daughter had joined the family. Marion Hall had embarked on a passionate affair with an Army Major and young Archibald had begun to self-style himself as Roy Hall.

Throughout the Halls' brief stay in Catterick, stories emerged of Archibald 'Roy' Hall attempting to blacken the character of his mother's new paramour. Hall documented this in several newspaper articles and his own autobiography but the stories varied and their validity is as intangible as the man himself. However, the Hall family rapidly found themselves back in Glasgow under a dark cloud.

Over the next few years, Hall emerged from his cocoon, enjoying a homosexual relationship with a Polish officer billeted with his family. As the war progressed, life on the home front for the young Hall consisted of charity box scams, wasted hours in the cinema dreaming of an exciting new life in America and efforts to embrace his newfound bisexual nature. In 1943, Roy Hall made the acquittance of Vic Oliver,[82] famous throughout Britain for headlining the radio show *Hi, Gang* and as the son-in-law of Prime Minister Winston Churchill. Easy sexual attraction prompted Hall to make the move to London and, over the next few years, according to his own autobiography, Hall enjoyed a life of socialising with the great and the good of the day. From Olivier to Novello to Mountbatten, it appears that Hall inhabited a rarefied world, if only in his own mind. What is certain, though, is that Hall found himself back in Glasgow by 1945, when his criminal career truly began.

The essence of Hall's crime was simple. At the behest of Hall's mother, who was concerned that she had not seen an old lady who lived in the same block, Mrs Robertson, out and about, he and a neighbour checked on her. Receiving no reply at the property, Hall entered and discovered that the old woman was dead. Rather than alerting the authorities to the death, he made a cursory examination of the old lady's possessions and found two shoeboxes crammed full of money hidden in a wardrobe. By this time, another neighbour – a tram driver named McLaughlin – had found his way into the home of Mrs Robertson. They ascertained that the boxes contained around £2,000 (equivalent to over £88,000 today) and Hall convinced his new cohort that they should leave around £100 in one of the boxes and divide the rest of the proceeds equally.

However, this crime heralded a recurring theme for Hall that haunted him for the next thirty years. As a career criminal, Hall was never quite able to transfer his audacious plans into successful conclusions. Unbeknownst to Hall, his partner in crime, McLaughlin, suffered from dipsomania and, while inebriated, would happily tell anyone about the crime. It did not take long for the police to become involved and Hall found himself in real fear of losing his liberty. However, this was not an open and shut case. The mental assessment Hall had undergone while at Catterick raised serious concerns with the local authorities and it was deemed appropriate to have him mentally evaluated.

Throughout the remainder of his life, Hall asserted that he was able to dupe the medical profession into sending him to Woodilee Home[83] on a false diagnosis of being mentally disturbed, thus avoiding a mandatory prison sentence.

Yet a far more plausible and valid scenario is that the medical professions of the day, both in Catterick and Glasgow, discovered a deep-seated psychological abnormality in his character.

Upon release from the institution in 1949, Archibald 'Roy' Hall underwent another transformation and became the more erudite Roy Fontaine. This was a nod to the silver screen and the work of Hitchcock and Joan Fontaine in Daphne Du Maurier's *Rebecca*. Despite inhabiting an almost Walter Mitty type of world, Hall was not distracted from his predilection for crime. By 1950, he had re-entered the penal system at Glasgow's notorious Barlinnie Prison. This proved a particularly difficult time for Hall – neither his upper-class manner nor his sexual tendencies enabled him to undertake his sentence with any real sense of security, despite his location.

During his time in prison, he became friends with an Englishman named John Wooton, who was incarcerated for attempting to defraud the country house where he was employed as a butler. Despite each man having quite different character traits, their friendship was sealed by an overwhelming need to achieve what they viewed as a better life. Wootton's experience masquerading as a butler gave Hall a burgeoning idea to transform himself into the perfect butler. Armed with copies of *Burke's Peerage* and *Roberts' Guide for Butlers and Other Household Staff* Fontaine used the remainder of his jail term to educate himself on etiquette, antiques and the duties of a butler, which would furnish him with the ideal skills to become a family retainer.

Hall was released from prison in 1951 and spent the next five years fleeting between working as a butler and robbing his employers. He was engaged to work for the affluent Lord and Lady Warren-Connel in their mansion house near the village of Balfron, Stirlingshire.

Such was the impertinence of the man that, while they were holidaying abroad, he borrowed their Bentley car and attended a lavish reception at Holyrood Palace. For good measure, he also plundered an antique shop.

Assiduously passing himself off as a rich American or member of the British aristocracy, Hall lived a Jekyll and Hyde existence as a confidence trickster and gentleman thief. Yet in 1956 the wheels came crashing off his nefarious activities and, over the following twenty years, he bounced in and out of prison, all the time refining his carefully created façade until he truly was an accomplished butler.

The final denouement of Archibald Hall's criminal life began upon his release from prison in 1977. By then, he was over fifty years of age. His mother Marion had passed away and David Barnard, the man Hall would refer to as his only true love, had been killed in a car crash. Perhaps the realisation of years wasted in prison and the loss of his only profoundly important relationships galvanised Hall into a new sense of urgency – an impetus to get what he wanted from life at any cost.

As Hall's new endeavours got underway, he returned to what he knew best – the life of a butler. He returned to the arms of his mistress, Irishwoman Mary Coggle, and it did not take him long to gain employment with Lady Margaret Hudson, the septuagenarian widow of a Tory M.P. who lived at Kirtleton House in rural Dumfriesshire. Life in this rural idyll changed in November 1977 when Hall's former lover, David Wright, visited Kirtleton House and, on a whim, Lady Hudson offered him a position as gardener on the estate. Such an arrangement was never going to work as Wright soon began to steal from Lady Hudson, incensing Hall.

Acutely aware that Wright was unpredictable and prone to drunken outbursts, Hall formulated a plan to protect his own secret and rid himself of Wright for good. The next day Hall suggested that they should go out shooting in the woods. Once Wright had discharged all his ammunition, Hall promptly shot him in the back of the head, for good measure adding another five bullets. The body was hidden in a grave in Pokeskinesike Burn, three quarters of a kilometre from Kirtleton House. Wright's absence was put down to his having taken a job elsewhere.

Although he had just committed murder, Hall's criminal past as a thief initially reached the attention of Lady Hudson and he was summarily dismissed. This presented no great difficulty to Hall – less than three months later he was back in the metropolis of London, gainfully employed as butler to Walter Scott-Elliot and his wife Dorothy at their fashionable Sloane Square residence. Hall took little time to ingratiate himself with his new employers and found that Captain Walter Scott-Elliot was particularly reliant on his services because of his advancing years and deteriorating health.

Scott-Elliot was now in his early eighties and had amassed a considerable personal fortune over the course of his lifetime. Emerging from distinguished military service at the end of the First World War, Scott-Elliot embarked on a career as a managing director of East Indian merchants. After his time in the commercial sector, he decided to direct his efforts towards public life and became a Labour M.P. in 1945. By the early 1950s, Scott-Elliot had returned to the business world and, alongside his Indian-born wife Dorothy (60), he built up a property portfolio with homes in Rome, London and Nice and a family estate in Dumfriesshire.

Hall was acutely aware that the personal collection of the Scott-Elliots included priceless items of jewellery and antiques, which offered him the scope to carry out the perfect robbery. After reacquainting himself with his old lover, Mary Coggle, it was only a matter of time before a third wheel would enter proceedings.

This emerged in the person of Michael Kitto (39), a petty thief on the run from the police after stealing £1000 from his employer. Hall and Kitto soon established a firm friendship and became lovers. They began to plan to rob the Scott-Elliots. On the evening of 8th December 1977, Hall and Kitto returned to the flat of his employers and spent several hours in his room getting drunk. Once they had exhausted their supply of liquor, they decided to obtain extra supplies from the flat's main cocktail cabinet. The men were shocked to be confronted by Dorothy Scott-Elliot, who demanded to know who Kitto was.

Without the slightest thought, both men took hold of Dorothy Scott-Elliot and, through a combination of suffocation and manual strangulation, ended the woman's life. Aghast at his ineptitude, Hall formulated a plan that he thought would allow him to defraud the estate of the Scott-Elliots and cover up the victims of the crime. In a macabre course of events, Archibald Hall recruited Mary Coggle to impersonate Mrs Scott-Elliot and, with an insensible Walter Scott-Elliot heavily medicated with sleeping pills, they began a nightmare odyssey, taking Hall back home to Scotland.

They reached Braco in Perthshire, where Dorothy Scott-Elliot's body was discarded. Unfortunately for Hall and his associates, the ground was frozen solid and they could only make a makeshift grave, covering the victim with branches and undergrowth. Hall kept hold of Walter Scott-Elliot, still heavily sedated, for a further two days. During brief moments of lucidity, Hall would get him to sign blank cheques. On 14th December 1977, the travelling party reached a particularly isolated area close to Glen Affric, situated south west of the village of Cannich in the Scottish Highlands. Hall decided that Walter Scott-Elliot had become surplus to requirements and the elderly man was slain. The frail eighty-two-year-old was strangled and had his throat crushed by the weight of Hall's boot. Finally, a shovel was used to crush his head. With each murder committed, the ferocity and torturous methods of death were intensifying and, in less than a year, Hall had become a serial killer.

Although Hall's criminal activities were rapidly drawing to a treacherous conclusion, several twists and turns remained to unfold. The following day, an argument erupted between Hall and Mary Coggle, who desperately wanted to keep the mink coat and expensive jewellery that had aided her disguise as Dorothy Scott-Elliot. Both Hall and Kitto were against this idea and wanted to get rid of the evidence but Coggle would not bend to their will. Working in tandem, Hall and Kitto overpowered Coggle, hit her over the head with a poker, and suffocated her with a plastic bag, before dumping her body in a stream between Glasgow and Carlisle.

Returning to the home of the Scott-Elliots for the final time, Hall and Kitto removed jewellery, cash and antiques from the property and, over Christmas 1977, they made further plans to split their gains. Hall must have imagined that his efforts were at last coming to fruition but this was not to be the case. At this point, his younger half-brother Donald appeared on the scene – a reintroduction that would prove to be Hall's ultimate downfall. Despite Hall's deeply flawed character and newfound murderous tendencies, he appeared to take the moral high ground with his brother. Donald was a dullard – a petty thief who had recently been released from Perth Prison for assaulting young girls. There was no family sentiment between the brothers and it appears that Hall genuinely loathed his sibling.

Despite possessing a less than penetrating intellect, Donald was cognisant that his brother and Kitto appeared to be financially well off and he took to being his brother's shadow. While staying in a rented bolthole near Carlisle, Hall again realised that there was a gap in his plan that needed to be closed. On 14th January 1978, Hall, Kitto and Donald were drinking in the Joiner's Arms pub. Donald was soon heavily inebriated and boasting to the pub's clientele that he and his brother were heading to Scotland to make a 'big score'.

On returning to the rented property, Hall made sure that his brother drank even more alcohol. While trying to impress his older brother, Donald's fate was sealed. Instructing Hall and Kitto to tie him up with six inches of string, he demonstrated a new skill. Donald sat on the floor and directed his brother and Kitto to tie his thumbs behind his back, then push his feet between his wrists, preventing any type of movement. Hall and Kitto moved into action and managed to place a cloth laced with chloroform over Donald's mouth. He fell into unconsciousness and was carried to the bathroom, where they drowned him in the bath.

The next day Hall and Kitto undertook another journey, heading towards the Scottish Borders and the A1, the main east coast artery between Scotland and England. Unfortunately for Hall and Kitto, they found themselves in snowy weather and decided to spend the night in the small East Lothian town of North Berwick. The decision was influenced by their need for a good night's sleep and to avoid the possibility of becoming snowbound in their car, not because Donald's body was in the boot.

Finding accommodation for the evening at the Blenheim House Hotel, the two men thought that they would be able to relax. They posed as brothers but the manager of the hotel, Norman Wright, found their story of catching a flight to Australia the next day improbable – he felt it more likely that they were confidence trickster who would not settle their bill the following day. Mr Wright discerned from Hall and Kitto's car that the vehicle registration did not match the road fund licence displayed in the car's front window. Wright immediately alerted the police to his concerns and the local constabulary made a search of the men's hotel room, where they discovered an envelope containing seventy-six silver Edwardian coins. Such was the arrogance of Archibald Hall that he requested that he and his brother be allowed to finish their evening meal before accompanying the officers to North

Berwick Police Station. At this time, the police were unaware of the body in the boot of the car and acquiesced with Hall's request.

Blenheim House Hotel, North Berwick, circa 2016.
Scene of Hall & Kitto's arrest.
Image Source: Public Domain.

As they were preparing to leave, Hall asked to use the bathroom in the hotel and promptly escaped out of the window, hailed a passing taxi and was spirited away towards Edinburgh. The police subsequently discovered the corpse of Donald Hall wrapped in a plastic sheet in the boot of the car. Thankfully, the police quickly apprehended Hall at a nearby roadblock and he was duly returned to North Berwick.

Under caution, Kitto made a full and frank confession and detailed the killings of the Scott-Elliots, Mary Coggle and Donald Hall. At first Hall denied any culpability but, on reflection, he decided that he had no choice but to tell the authorities the whole story as the game was up. He summarily admitted his guilt and added in the slaying of David Wright for good measure. Mary Coggle's unidentified remains had already been discovered but, even with the help of Hall and Kitto, several hundred police officers had to carry out a prolonged search over several days before the bodies were discovered.

Throughout the months that followed, Hall never appeared to display any kind of emotion. His interviews with Lothian and Borders Police were highly professional and revealed a full insight into his criminal activities but the man himself was as elusive in character as ever. Despite Hall's continued outward bravado and newfound pleasure at becoming famous in the British press, he was acutely aware of the prison term that he was facing. Using tranquilizers that he had managed to conceal from the authorities, he attempted to commit suicide but to no avail.

In 1978, Archibald Hall, alias Roy Fontaine, and Michael Kitto pleaded guilty and each received two life sentences at the High Court in Edinburgh for the murders, which had occurred on Scottish soil. In September 1978 Hall and Kitto faced the Old Bailey and a charge of murdering Dorothy Scott-Elliot. The case proved to be an exercise in justice, Kitto was sentenced to a minimum of fifteen years and the court recommended that he should never be released.

Less than five years later, a new Home Office directive was introduced known as a 'whole life tariff', which noted that the most dangerous and pervasive threat of certain prisoners required a mechanism to hold them in prison for the remainder of their lives without direct intervention from the serving Home Secretary. This Category A listing has been applied to very few, who include the Yorkshire Ripper, the Moors Murderers, Dennis Nilsen and one Archibald Hall.

Over the course of the next twenty years and more, Hall made several aborted attempts to keep his name in the limelight through unsuccessful books, media interviews and failed suicides, and petitioned the Home Office for the right to die. In 1992, Kitto was released from incarceration and, in 1999, Archibald Hall published an autobiography, suitably entitled *A Perfect Gentleman*. In a complete work of fiction, Hall portrayed himself as a man who was forced into every criminal endeavour either by cohorts or by circumstance. At no point did he show sympathy for his victims or any type of repentance for his vicious crimes. Indeed, he boasted that he had carried out further murders, for which he had never faced justice.

On 16th September 2002, Hall was eagerly awaiting news on the contested issue of the whole life tariff as the European Court of Human Rights was in the process of debating its ethics. On that very day, though, he succumbed to the effects of a severe stroke at Kingston Prison, Portsmouth, and passed away. Less than a month after its protracted analysis, the European Court of Human Rights released their findings, stating that a sentence of a whole life tariff utilised in the United Kingdom was neither unmerciful nor unjustifiable.

❖ ❖ ❖

Endnotes

[1] Margaret (1283–1290) was the queen-designate of Scotland from 1286 until her death. As she was never crowned, her status as monarch is uncertain and has been vigorously debated. Margaret was the daughter of King Eric II of Norway and Margaret of Scotland. By the end of the reign of her maternal grandfather, Alexander III, who died in 1286, she was his only surviving descendant and recognised as heir apparent to the Scottish throne. Owing to her young age, Margaret remained in Norway rather than going to Scotland. She was finally sent to Scotland in September 1290 but died in the Orkney Isles on the journey from Norway.

[2] Edward I (1239–1307), also known as Edward Longshanks and the Hammer of the Scots – Latin: Malleus Scotorum – was King of England from 1272 to 1307. He was credited with many accomplishments during his reign, including restoring royal authority after the reign of Henry III, establishing Parliament as a permanent institution and a functional system for raising taxes, and reforming the law through statutes.

[3] John Balliol, John I of Scotland (1249–1314) was king from 1292 to 1296. Little is known of his early life. John abdicated at Stracathro, near Montrose, on 12th July 1296. Here, the arms of Scotland were formally torn from his surcoat, giving him the abiding name of 'Toom Tabard' (empty coat). John died in late 1314 at his family's chateau at Helicourt in France.

[4] The Auld Alliance was a treaty made in 1295 between Scotland and France for the purpose of controlling England's multiple invasions. In Scots, the word auld, meaning old, has become an affectionate term for the long-lasting association between the two countries.

[5] Andrew Murray lived from around 1270 to 1297. The Murrays were a family of Flemish descent who settled in Moray during the reign of David I. They were among the many families, mostly of French or Norman descent, invited from England by David I to help him establish his authority in the Gaelic-speaking areas of

Scotland.

[6] Sir William Wallace (c.1270–1305) was a Scottish knight who became one of the main leaders during the first war of Scottish independence. He was appointed Guardian of Scotland and served until his defeat at the Battle of Falkirk in July 1298. In August 1305 Wallace was captured in Robroyston, near Glasgow, and handed over to Edward Longshanks, who had him hanged, drawn and quartered.

[7] John Comyn III, (c. 1270–1306) was a man with links to both the Scottish and English royal families, and became a Guardian of Scotland at a crucial time. John Comyn III was also known as Sir John Comyn, John the Red, or just the Red Comyn, to distinguish him from his father, also John Comyn, who was referred to as the Black Comyn. The Black Comyn was one of the 'competitors' for the crown of Scotland. The Comyns were one of the most important families in Scotland. They were the Lords of Badenoch and the Earls of Buchan, and owned extensive estates elsewhere in the country.

[8] Sir Simon Fraser of Oliver and Neidpath was a Scottish knight who fought in the wars of Scottish independence, for which he was hanged, drawn and quartered in 1306. In 1303 at the Battle of Roslin. Fraser killed Ralph Manton, an English treasury clerk, whom Fraser accused of embezzling King Edward I of funds and neglecting to pay Fraser's wages when he was in English service. Consequently, King Edward I marched north. As Edward I approached Dunfermline, the Bishop of St Andrews and the Bishop of Glasgow, along with the Red Comyn, met his army and submitted. Fraser refused to swear fealty to the English king and did not attend.

[9] Robert I (1274–1329), popularly known as Robert the Bruce, was King of Scots from 1306 until his death in 1329. Robert was one of the most famous warriors of his generation and fought successfully during his reign to regain Scotland's place as an independent country.

[10] During the late twelfth and thirteenth centuries, small groups of

judges (often referred to as justices) were sent from the central courts at Westminster to all the counties of England, except Durham and Chester where the royal jurisdiction did not extend, to preside over local courts.

[11] Isabella MacDuff, Countess of Buchan (died c. 1314) was a distinct figure in the wars of Scottish independence. She was the daughter of Donnchadh III, Earl of Fife, and Johanna de Clare. After the Red Comyn was killed, Isabella's husband joined the English side, but Isabella took a contrary position.

[12] Donnchadh IV, Earl of Fife (1289–1353), was Guardian of Scotland and the last native Scottish ruler of Fife. He was born in the same year that his father was killed and became mormaer (a regional ruler, theoretically second only to the King of Scots) as a baby. He missed the crowning of Robert Bruce because of his captivity in England and Robert was forced to call upon Donnchadh's sister Isabella to officiate in his absence.

[13] Edward II (1284–1327), also known as Edward of Caernarfon, was King of England from 1307 until he was deposed in January 1327. Edward became heir apparent to the throne following the death of his elder brother Alphonso. From 1300, Edward accompanied his father on military campaigns against Scotland. He married Isabella, daughter of the powerful King Philip IV of France, in 1308, as part of a long-running effort to resolve tensions between the English and French crowns.

[14] In the early nineteenth century, Sir Walter Scott visited farms on both sides of the Scottish and English border and listened to the verse and chant to detail the romance of the reivers. There is extraordinarily little documented history on the Border Reivers, but there is a rich heritage of ballads and verse, which has been passed down through the farming communities of the Scottish Borders, Cumbria and Northumberland.

[15] Gilnockie comes from the Scottish Gaelic meaning 'Little White Hill.' It is situated near Canobie in modern-day Dumfries and Galloway.

[16] The surname Armstrong was common in Northumbria and the Scottish Borders. Its members became a powerful clan in Liddesdale and the 'Debatable Lands' (an area in constant flux as the distinct kingdoms of Scotland and England both claimed domain).

[17] 'Reive' is an early Anglo term meaning 'to rob', and is related to the old English verb 'reave', meaning to plunder.

[18] The Irish hobby horse is a now extinct breed of horse represented most closely today by the Connemara pony.

[19] A coat of mail, typically made of iron rings or plates attached to canvas or similar fabric.

[20] Robert Maxwell, fifth Lord Maxwell (1493–1546) was a member of the council of Regency (1536) of the Kingdom of Scotland, Regent of the Isle of Arran and patriarch of Clan Maxwell. A distinguished Scottish nobleman, politician, soldier and, in 1513, Lord High Admiral of Scotland's navy. Lord Maxwell was a member of the royal council of James V of Scotland. In 1537, he was one of the ambassadors sent to the French Court to negotiate the marriage of James to Mary of Guise, whom he espoused as proxy for the king.

[21] Lord Warden of the Marches was an office in the governments of England and Scotland. The holders were responsible for the security of the border between the two countries, and often took part in military action. They were also responsible, along with 'Conservators of the truce', for administering the special type of border law known as March Law. The Marches on both sides of the border were traditionally split into West, Middle and East, each with their own warden answerable to the Lord Warden-general. The English Western March was based at Carlisle and the Eastern March at Berwick-upon-Tweed.

[22] William Dacre, seventh Baron Greystock, later third Baron Dacre of Gilsland, was an English peer, a Cumberland landowner, and the holder of important offices under the Crown, including many years' service as Warden of the West Marches

[23] Adam Scott, Laird of Tushielaw along with his neighbour William Cockburn of Henderland, were convicted of high treason, theft and levying blackmail. They died on the scaffold. Another variation of the story notes that Cockburn of Henderland was caught by James V and hanged over his own castle door.

[24] Caerlanrig – also spelled 'Carlenrig' (Gaelic: Cathair Lannraig) is a hamlet in the parish of Cavers in the Scottish Borders, lying on the River Teviot, six miles (10 km) north east of that river's source, and ten miles (16 km) south west of Hawick.

[25] Many women retained their maiden name in Scotland on marriage, symbolising that they did not join their husband's kin, and marriages were intended to create friendship between kin groups, rather than new bonds of kinship.

[26] Sir Gilbert Elliot, second Baronet of Minto (1693–1766) was a Scottish lawyer, politician and judge. In June 1726, he was made a judge of the Court of Session, taking the judicial title Lord Minto. He became a Lord of Justiciary in 1733 and Keeper of the Signet in 1761. In 1763, he was promoted to Lord Justice Clerk.

Alexander Boswell, Lord Auchinleck (1706–1782), was a judge of the Supreme Courts of Scotland. He was the father of the author and biographer James Boswell and grandfather of the songwriter Sir Alexander Boswell. Alexander was nominated to the Court of Session in 1754, receiving the additional appointment to the High Court of Justiciary in the following year.

Andrew Pringle (died 1776) was a Scottish judge and Senator of the College of Justice. He passed the Scottish bar as an advocate in 1740 and became Sheriff of Wigtown in 1750. He then served as Sheriff of Selkirk from 1751 before becoming Solicitor General for Scotland, a position he held from 1755 to 1759.

Henry Home, Lord Kames (1696–1782) was a Scottish writer, philosopher, advocate, judge and agricultural improver. A central figure of the Scottish Enlightenment, a founding member of the Philosophical Society of Edinburgh, and active in the Select Society, he acted as patron to some of the most influential thinkers of the Scottish Enlightenment, including the philosopher David Hume.

James Fergus, Lord Pitfour (1700–1777), was a Scottish advocate and second Laird of Pitfour, a large estate in Buchan. His flourishing law practice was situated opposite Parliament House in Edinburgh. He became Dean of the Faculty of Advocates in 1760 and was elevated to the bench as Lord Pitfour in 1764.

George Broun of Coalston became an advocate on 31st January 1734. In 1748, he was appointed Sheriff Depute of the county of Forfar. On the death of Peter Wedderburn of Chesterhall, he was promoted to the bench and took his seat by the title of Lord Coalston on 18th December 1756. On the resignation of Alexander Fraser of Strichen, he was also nominated a Lord of Justiciary – on 18th January 1765. He resigned the latter appointment a short time before his death at Coalston on 6th November 1776.

Sir Thomas Miller, (1717–1789), known as Lord Barskimming (1766–1788) and Lord Glenlee (from 1788) during his judicial service, was a Scottish advocate, judge, politician and landowner. He was a founder member of the Royal Society of Edinburgh in 1783, and served as the society's first vice-president from 1783 to 1786.

[27] Sir James Montgomery, first Baronet Stanhope (1721–1803) was a Scottish advocate, judge, country landowner and politician, who sat in the House of Commons from 1766 to 1775. In 1783 he was a joint founder of the Royal Society of Edinburgh. Sir David Dalrymple, Lord Hailes, 3rd Baronet of Hailes (1726–1792) was a Scottish judge, advocate and historian born in Edinburgh.

[28] Lieutenant General Lord George Beauclerk (1704–1768) was a British Army officer and served in the 1st Regiment of Foot Guards. He was promoted to captain and lieutenant colonel in September 1736. In 1745 he was nominated aide-de-camp to King George II with the rank of colonel, and in 1747 he obtained the colonelcy of the 8th Regiment of Marines. In 1753 he was appointed Governor of Landguard Fort, holding the post until his death. He was promoted to the rank of major general in 1755, to

Lieutenant General in 1758, and Commander in Chief in Scotland from 1756 to 1767.

[29] The High Court of Justiciary is the supreme court in Scotland. The High Court is both a trial court and a court of appeal. Article XIX of the Treaty of Union, which united Scotland and England into Great Britain, preserved the High Court of Justiciary, though the High Court became subject to the Parliament of Westminster, which could enact '...regulations for the better administration of Justice'. Despite Westminster appearing to have appellate jurisdiction through the judicial function of the House of Lords, this appears to have had little effect in practice. In 1713 a case (Magistrates of Elgin v. Ministers of Elgin) was heard by the House of Lords, which overturned a decision made by the High Court. However, in 1781, the House of Lords resolved that there could be no appeal from the High Court, as no right of appeal existed beyond the Court following the Treaty of Union.

[30] Adam Gillies, Lord Gillies (1766–1842), became an advocate in 1787. From 1806, he was sheriff-depute of Kincardineshire. From 1811 to 1842, he was a senator of the College of Justice, based in Edinburgh. Gillies married Elizabeth Carnegy, and, from 1811, their niece Margaret (1803–1887) and Mary Gillies (1800–1870) came to live with them from London. The girls were educated by Lord and Lady Gillies and introduced into Edinburgh society. During their time in Edinburgh, they were introduced to Thomas Southwood Smith, the powerful new preacher to the Unitarian congregation at Skinners' Hall in the Canongate, Edinburgh. He was to play a large part in their later lives. Gillies retired because of ill health and died on 24th December 1842.

[31] Nailor: A person who made nails by hand. Principally employed to maintain the teeth (nails) on the carding machine used on wool and cotton before weaving.

[32] Originally the site of the Council House. Built in 1812 by French prisoners of war, a courtroom was added in 1861 to the designs of the Edinburgh architect David Rhind. Sir Walter Scott, who made his first appearance as a defence lawyer here in 1793, often visited

the previous court building. A plaque (on the Market Place side of the building) dating from 1932 commemorates the centenary of Scott's death. The building is still used as a court and justice is regularly dispensed from here.

[33] The regiment was raised in Argyll by General Duncan Campbell of Lochnell for John Campbell, 5th Duke of Argyll, as the 98th Argyllshire Highlanders, Regiment of Foot, a line regiment of the British Army, in 1794 in response to the threat posed by the French Revolution. The regiment lost its territorial designation and was renamed the 91st Regiment of Foot in April 1809. The 1st Battalion then took part in the disastrous Walcheren campaign in autumn 1809. By 1814 the regiment had seen action at the Battle of Orthez in February 1814 and the Battle of Toulouse in April 1814.

[34] The Friends of the People was an organisation created by the Whig Party in 1792 in Great Britain that was focused on advocating for parliamentary reform. While in England the society drew its membership from an exclusive aristocratic set. Its Scottish subscription was derived from a far broader socio-economic group.

[35] Theobald Wolfe Tone, posthumously known as Wolfe Tone (1763–1798) was a leading Irish revolutionary figure and one of the founding members of the United Irishmen, a republican society that revolted against British rule in Ireland. He led the group going into the 1798 Irish Rebellion. Tone requested a military death by firing squad but this was denied on the grounds that he had been found guilty of treason and had forfeited his rights as a soldier. Tone was taken to his cell and cut his own throat with a penknife on 12th November 1798 to deny the British the satisfaction of hanging him. Tone survived for seven days before passing away from the self-inflicted wound.

[36] Common Haugh: A public area of ground. Normally level and situated by the banks of a river.

[37] St Boswells is a unique Scottish Borders town with the largest village green in Scotland. The Green is the venue for an annual fair held each year on 18th July, dating back to the 1600s. This has

been held since 1743. It was originally a sheep fair lasting seven days and, by the 1820s, became a one-day event, expanding to include cattle and horses. Over 1,000 horses were offered for sale each year in the early 1900s. Today this kind of event is often referred to as a horse fair.

[38] Bridget Ennis (21) and Bridget Butterly (19) were both imprisoned in Kilmainham Gaol, Dublin, in 1821. They were convicted of the killing of a young lady, Miss Thompson, who lived in the house in which Bridget Butterly had been a servant.

[39] The *Police Gazette* or *Hue and Cry* was published in Dublin every Tuesday and Friday by Alexander Thom & Co., and is almost always referred to as *Hue and Cry* It is unclear when *Hue and Cry* was first published in Ireland and exactly how much of the publication survives.

[40] Turnkey: A nineteenth-century term for a prison warden or gaol keeper.

[41] Footpad thieves committed the same crimes as highwaymen – robbing 'on the king's highway' – and the main distinction between them was the presence of horses: highwaymen were mounted on horses and robbed people travelling in coaches, whereas footpads and street robbers moved on foot and robbed people travelling on foot.

[42] The County Gaol of Down was opened in 1796. Built and administered by the County Grand Jury of Down, the gaol-housed prisoners had been convicted of a wide variety of offences. During its period of operation (1796–1830) the gaol saw many changes in attitudes to crime and punishment. Georgian gaols were notoriously unregulated and haphazard in their operation of prison legislation. As the eighteenth century gave way to the nineteenth, the gaol became increasingly outmoded and unable to implement increasing bureaucracy and stricter attitudes to separating classes of criminals. The gaol closed in 1830.

[43] Trepanning is a surgical intervention in which a hole is drilled or scraped into the human skull. The intentional perforation of the

cranium exposes the dura mater to treat health problems related to intracranial diseases or release pressured blood build-up from an injury.

[44] George Combe (1788–1858) was a trained Scottish lawyer and a spokesman of the phrenological movement for two decades. He founded the Edinburgh Phrenological Society in 1820 and wrote a noted study, The Constitution of Man (1828). After his marriage in 1833, Combe took to promoting phrenology internationally in his later years.

[45] David Hume (1711–1776) was a Scottish historian, economist, librarian, essayist and philosopher of the Scottish Enlightenment. He is best known for his influential system of philosophical scepticism, naturalism and empiricism.

Adam Smith (1723–1790) was a Scottish economist and philosopher. Known as the 'the Father of Economics' he penned two classical titles 'The Theory of Moral Sentiments' (1759) and 'An Inquiry into the Nature and Causes of the Wealth of Nations' (1776). Nations is considered the first modern work of economics.

James Burnett, Lord Monboddo (1714–1799) was a Scottish philosopher, judge, deist and founder of modern comparative historical linguistics.

[46] William Henry Playfair (1790–1857) was a prominent Scottish architect in the nineteenth century, who designed the Eastern, or Third, New Town in Edinburgh and many of its neoclassical landmarks.

[47] Robert Knox (1791–1862) was a Scottish anatomist and ethnologist. He was a lecturer on anatomy in Edinburgh and obtained cadavers for dissection through erroneous methods after the passage of the Anatomy Act in 1832, which gave free licence to doctors, teachers of anatomy and medical students to dissect donated bodies.

[48] William Burke and William Hare were resurrectionists, or body snatchers, who carried out a series of sixteen murders over a period of about ten months in 1828 in Edinburgh. They then sold the

corpses to Robert Knox for dissection at his anatomy lectures.

[49] Colonel William Ivison Macadam (1856–1902) was a prominent Scottish scientist (analytical chemist), academic author and antiquarian. He was also Colonel of the First Lothian Volunteer Infantry Brigade and a leading Freemason. He was generally known by his middle name, Ivison.

[50] In 1902 Colonel Macadam was appointed commander of the Second Scottish Volunteer Coronation Battalion for Edward VII's coronation. Macadam's career as a Voluntary army officer extended over a twenty-seven-year period.

[51] Elison Ann Macadam (1862–1965) became the first woman to graduate in chemistry at King's College London. After her graduation, Elison worked in the chemical laboratory as Assistant to Professor A. K. Huntington, Professor of Metallurgy at King's. Later, her daughter Rosalind Desch (1913–1994) carried on this tradition of women in education and went on to build The Study School into a leading all-girls school in Wimbledon, London. Prior to her death, Rosalind saw that the school's future was protected by making it over into a charitable education foundation.

[52] Sir Ivison Stevenson Macadam (1894–1974) was the first Director General of the Royal Institute of International Affairs and the founding President of the National Union of Students. He served in World War One and was the youngest major in the British Army as Officer Commanding Royal Engineers, Archangel, North Russian Expeditionary Force – the ill-fated Allied military campaign of 1918–1919 following the armistice with Germany, and the final major military action of WWI.

[53] Stevenson Macadam (1829–1901) was a Scottish scientist, analytical chemist, lecturer, and academic author who lectured at the Royal College of Surgeons, Edinburgh and Edinburgh University. He was a founding member of the Institute of Chemistry of Great Britian and President of The Royal Scottish Society.

[54] Sophia Louisa Jex-Blake (1840–1912) was an English physician,

teacher and feminist. She led the campaign to secure women access to a university education when she and six other women, collectively known as the 'Edinburgh Seven', began studying medicine at Edinburgh University in 1869. She was the first practising female doctor in Scotland, and one of the first in the UK. She was involved in founding two medical schools for women – in London and Edinburgh – at a time when no other medical schools were training women.

[55] The Edinburgh College of Medicine for Women was established by Elsie Inglis with the support of her father John Inglis, who had been a senior civil servant in India. On his return to Edinburgh he became a supporter of medical education for women, and used his influence to help establish the college. The college was founded in 1889 at a time when women were not admitted to university medical schools in the UK. Elsie Inglis went on to become a leader in the suffrage movement and to found the Scottish Women's Hospital organisation in World War One.

[56] Sir Henry Duncan Littlejohn (1826–1914) was a Scottish surgeon, public health official and forensic scientist. Littlejohn served for over forty-five years as Edinburgh's first medical officer, during which time he brought about marked improvements in the living conditions and health of the city's inhabitants. He also served as a police surgeon and medical adviser in Scottish criminal cases.

[57] Dr George Robert Wilson (1866–1908) a native of Duns and former Scottish rugby player, was educated at Edinburgh University. After a period as Deputy Superintendent at the Royal Edinburgh Asylum he became Superintendent of Mavisbank Asylum, a position he held until 1905. The noted clinician retired to dedicate himself to the treatment of nervous conditions. His published work included Clinical Studies in Vice & Insanity (1899).

[58] Mavisbank House was commissioned by Sir John Clerk of Penicuik, one of the leading figures of the Scottish Enlightenment, and designed by Clerk with William Adam, father of the Adam

brothers and the leading architect of early eighteenth-century Scotland. It was constructed in the 1720s. Mavisbank continued to be owned by members of the Clerk family until 1814 and alterations to the house and policies were undertaken in the early nineteenth century. In 1877, the house, with numerous additions and extensions, was used as a lunatic asylum. The hospital closed in 1953 and was bought by its last medical superintendent, Dr Harrowes. Mr Archie Stevenson subsequently bought Mavisbank in the late 1950's and it was gutted by fire in 1973. After his death, ownership was uncertain and, sadly, it has remained derelict ever since.

[59] Sir John Batty Tuke (1835–1913) was one of the most influential psychiatrists in Scotland in the late nineteenth century, and a Unionist (MP) from 1900 to 1910. His career in Edinburgh from 1863 to 1910 spanned a period of significant social and political changes in asylum governance and care in Scotland. His professional success in public and private practice and his powerful role in several prominent medical societies allowed him to influence his colleagues towards a more physiological understanding of mental illness and its treatment.

[60] Scotus was a Scottish Catholic priest and Franciscan friar, university professor, philosopher and theologian. His complex and nuanced thought, which earned him the nickname 'the Subtle Doctor', left an indelible mark on discussions of such disparate topics as the semantics of religious language, the complexity of universals, divine illumination and the concept of human freedom.

[61] Duns motto: Duns dings [batters, beats down, defeats;] a.

[62] The 1639 and 1640 Bishops' Wars were the first of the conflicts known collectively as the 1638–1651 Wars of the Three Kingdoms, which occurred in England, Scotland and Wales. The wars originated in disputes over governance of the Church of Scotland that began in the 1580s and reached a breaking point when Charles I attempted to force a uniform code of practices on the Kirk and Church of England in 1637.

[63] Familicide is a type of murder or murder-suicide in which a

perpetrator kills multiple close family members in quick succession, most often children, relatives, spouse, siblings, or parents. In half the cases, the killer lastly kills themselves in a murder-suicide.

[64] Chesting: A Scottish term describing the act of placing the deceased in their coffin.

[65] Work on the Oban Hydro commenced but was abandoned and left to fall into disrepair after 1882 when Dr Orr, the scheme's originator, realised he had grossly underestimated its cost. Work on McCaig's Tower started in 1895. Paid for by John Stewart McCaig (1824–1902), construction ceased in 1902 on the death of its benefactor.

[66] John Glaister (1856–1932) was a graduate of the university who became Regius Professor of Forensic Medicine and Public Health from 1898 to 1931. During more than thirty years at the university, Glaister introduced postgraduate degrees for a BSc and a DSc in Public Health and opened modern laboratories for both Public Health and Forensic Medicine. He became famous for his appearances as an expert witness in famous legal cases such as the murder trial of Oscar Slater in 1909.

[67] Robert Munro, first Baron Alness (28 May 1868–6 October 1955) was a Scottish lawyer, judge and Liberal politician. He served as Secretary for Scotland in Lloyd George's coalition government and as Lord Justice Clerk between 1922 and 1933. Other famous cases include that of Donald Merrett – a murder charge not proven on direction from Lord Alness.

[68] On 9th January 1923 in Holloway Prison, twenty-nine-year-old Edith Thompson collapsed in terror at the prospect of her hanging. Heavily sedated by the governor, she was carried to the gallows by four prison warders. Thompson was hanged for her part in the murder of her husband Percy. On 3rd October 1922, the Thompsons attended a performance at the Criterion Theatre in London's Piccadilly Circus along with Edith's uncle and aunt, Mr and Mrs J. Laxton. They left the theatre at eleven o'clock and all went to Piccadilly Circus tube station, where they separated. The

Thompsons caught the 11.30 pm train to Ilford. As they walked along Belgrave Road, a man jumped out from behind some bushes near their home and attacked Percy. After a violent struggle, during which Edith Thompson was knocked to the ground, Percy was stabbed. Mortally wounded, he died before Edith could summon help. In Pentonville Prison, twenty-year-old Frederick Bywaters, who had tried since his arrest to save his lover Thompson from execution, was himself hanged. The two executions occurred simultaneously at nine o'clock in the morning, about half a mile apart.

[69] Jessie King lived with her partner Michael Pearson in lodgings at Canonmills, Edinburgh and ran a small baby farming business. One of the children in her care was a baby boy named Alexander Gunn who disappeared. At this point to evade further investigation Jessie moved to the Stockbridge area of the city where she began looking after a baby girl who promptly vanished. It is highly likely that Jessie would have avoided justice had it not been for the discovery of the body of a male baby by some young boys who were playing in the Stockbridge area. Jessie was interviewed by the police and broke down during questioning. Leading the authorities to the cellar they discovered the remains of a female baby. Jessie was charged with both murders and went on trial for Alexander's killing in February 1889. She told the court that she had murdered Alexander in a state of 'drunken melancholy.' In the case of the baby girl she had administered whisky to make the child sleep, but claimed that she had 'overdone it.' Jessie was found guilty and sentenced to death. While awaiting execution she was examined by a medical commission at Calton Jail who concluded that she was legally sane. She was hanged by James Barry at 8 am on Monday 11th March 1889.

[70] The General Strike was called on 3rd May 1926. It lasted nine days and represented a historic walkout by British workers, representing the dissatisfaction of millions of blue-collar workers and ushering in change across the United Kingdom. It was called by the Trades Union Congress in response to poor working conditions and reduced pay. This became one of the largest

industrial disputes in British history, with millions of people participating in the nine-day strike in which working men established a new solidarity. The General Strike was identified as not protected by the Trade Disputes Act of 1906, except for the coal industry, meaning that the unions became liable for the decision to breach contracts. By 12th May, the TUC General Council met at Downing Street to declare that the strike was being called off with the agreement that no striker would be victimised for their decision, despite the government having no power over employer's decisions. In 1927, the Trade Disputes Act was introduced by Stanley Baldwin, banning any sympathy strikes or mass picketing. his act is still in force today.

[71] *No Mean City* is based on the notes of Alexander McArthur. The novel was co-written by Kingsley Long, a London journalist assigned the task of translating the notes into a publishable novel. The graphic descriptions of violence, drunkenness and poverty shocked many in polite society.

[72] On 24th November 1928 George Geddes was drowned while trying to save a man who had jumped off King's Bridge into the River Clyde. George Geddes, David Docherty and Constable Thirsk rushed out in a boat towards the man in the water, near the suspension bridge. George and David were rowing double scull when the boat was turned round by the eddy in the heavy current. They missed the man drifting by so George dived into the water but both men went under. Constable Thirsk tried to take George's oars but the boat was being whirled around by the current. George appeared on the surface near to the barges, then, a few minutes later, appeared at the bridge again, the pressure of the current almost lifting him out to his waist. He slid back into the water and disappeared. Both George and the suicide victim perished. George Geddes' body was discovered some four days later.

[73] The Royal Humane Society was founded in London in 1774 by two eminent medical men, William Hawes and Thomas Cogan, who were keen to promote resuscitation techniques. It became apparent that people were putting their own lives in danger rescuing others and awards were given in recognition of these acts

of bravery. This remains the purpose of the society today. George Geddes assisted his father as an assistant officer of the society.

[74] The New Central Police Office in Low Green Street (now Turnbull Street) opened as headquarters of the Glasgow Police on 23rd March 1906.

[75] Professor Glaister, as noted in previous chapter.

[76] A Queen's Counsel (QC) is an advocate appointed by the monarch to be one of 'Her Majesty's Counsel learned in the law' – the role is described as the King's Counsel (KC) when the monarch is male. The independent bar in Scotland is known as the Faculty of Advocates and its members are designated as advocates. The position was not recognised before 1868 and initially was reserved for law officers, including the Lord Advocate and Solicitor General for Scotland – thereafter the Dean of the Faculty of Advocates. In 1897 a petition by the Faculty of Advocates for the establishment of a Scottish roll of QC was approved, and the first appointments were made later that year.

[77] George Lewis MacFarlane, Lord Ormidale LLD (1854–1941) was a nineteenth/twentieth-century Scottish law lord who served as a senator of the College of Justice.

[78] The Criminal Appeal (Scotland) Act 1926 introduced a power for the High Court of Justiciary to allow appeal on the basis of new evidence not heard at the original trial. An appeal on these grounds would succeed only where the court was satisfied that, had the jury heard the additional evidence, they would have been bound to acquit and that a verdict in the absence of the additional evidence amounted to a miscarriage of justice.

[79] Dr Heide holds the rank of Professor of Criminology at the University of South Florida. Professor Heide enjoys teaching both undergraduate and graduate students and is actively engaged in thesis and doctoral advising. Dr Heide is the recipient of six awards for teaching excellence, including USF's most prestigious award – the Jerome Krivanek Distinguished Teacher Award. Professor Heide's publication record includes four books and over

120 other professional publications in the areas of adolescent homicide, parricide, family violence, personality assessment and juvenile justice.

[80] The tradition of gang formation in Glasgow stretched back at least to the 1880s, and gang rivalries appear to have derived a momentum of their own during the late nineteenth century, irrespective of short-term economic trends, both in Glasgow and in other British municipalities. Religious sectarianism had been rife in Scotland for centuries; however, the centre of modern religious intolerance evolved in Glasgow. Originally, Glasgow was mainly Protestant, but in the nineteenth and twentieth centuries, large numbers of Irish Catholic immigrants came to the west coast of Scotland, drawn by jobs in local industries in Scotland.

[81] Thelema is an esoteric and occult social or spiritual philosophy and new religious movement developed in the early 1900s by Alister Crowley, an English writer, mystic and ceremonial magician.

[82] Victor Oliver von Samek (1898–1964) was an Austrian-born actor and radio comedian. Born in Vienna, the son of Baron Viktor von Samek, he studied medicine at Vienna University but abandoned it for his first love – music. For a time he studied under Mahler. During the First World War he served in the Austrian cavalry. After the war he worked as a banker and textile manufacturer before returning to music. In 1926 he visited the United States as a conductor and violinist. Discovering a talent for light comedy while working in America, he became most famous for appearing in the BBC radio show Hi, Gang. Oliver married Winston Churchill's daughter, Sarah, in 1936. The union proved relatively brief, due in part to Churchill's disapproval of the union.

[83] Woodilee Hospital was a psychiatric institution situated in Lenzie, East Dunbartonshire, Glasgow. It offered mental health provision for the people of Glasgow and surrounding areas over a period of more than 100 years.

Printed in Great Britain
by Amazon